A Sustainable Future

ISSUES

Volume 218

Series Editor

Lisa Firth

Independence

Educational Publishers

Cambridge

First published by Independence

The Studio, High Green

Great Shelford

Cambridge CB22 5EG

England

© Independence 2012

British Library Cataloguing in Publication Data

A sustainable future. -- (Issues ; 218)

1. Nature--Effect of human beings on. 2. Environmental

responsibility. 3. Sustainability.

I. Series II. Firth, Lisa.

363.7-dc23

ISBN-13: 978 1 86168 603 9

Printed in Great Britain

MWL Print Group Ltd

CONTENTS

Chapter 1 Sustainable Resources

Chapter 2 Safeguarding the Natural World

Chapter 3 People and the Environment

OTHER TITLES IN THE ISSUES SERIES

For more on these titles, visit: www.independence.co.uk

A note on critical evaluation

Because the information reprinted here is from a number of different sources, readers should bear in mind the origin of the text and whether the source is likely to have a particular bias when presenting information (just as they would if undertaking their own research). It is hoped that, as you read about the many aspects of the issues explored in this book, you will critically evaluate the information presented. It is important that you decide whether you are being presented with facts or opinions. Does the writer give a biased or an unbiased report? If an opinion is being expressed, do you agree with the writer?

A Sustainable Future offers a useful starting point for those who need convenient access to information about the many issues involved. However, it is only a starting point. Following each article is a URL to the relevant organisation's website, which you may wish to visit for further information.

The environment

The natural world is fragile, and needs care, respect and knowledge from all people.

What is it?

Your surroundings, and how they influence your development. The environment is the complex set of physical, geographic, biological, social, cultural and political conditions that surround an individual or organism and that ultimately determine its form and the nature of its survival.

The environment influences how people live and how societies develop. For that reason, people, progress, economic development and the environment are closely linked.

The environment can also pose risks. Air pollution, waterborne diseases, toxic chemicals and natural disasters are some of the challenges the environment presents for mankind.

The environment influences how people live and how societies develop

Natural resources, land, water and forests are being degraded at an alarming rate in many countries – and once they are gone, they are irreplaceable!

For development to be sustainable – meeting the needs of the present without compromising the ability of future generations to meet theirs – countries must take into account environmental concerns in addition to economic progress.

Concern for a sound global environment is essential to fighting poverty, as the poorest people tend to live in the most vulnerable places.

Why should I care?

Each year around the world:

⇨ Three million people die prematurely from waterborne diseases.

⇨ About 400,000 children under five die from diarrhoea in India alone.

⇨ Around 1.6 million people die from exposure to cooking stove smoke inside their homes. About half of these deaths occur in India and China. Most victims are children and women from poor rural families who lack access to safe water, sanitation and modern household fuels.

⇨ A million people die from malaria, mostly in Sub-Saharan African countries.

⇨ A million people die from urban air pollution.

⇨ Respiratory infections, diarrhoea and malaria account for more than 20% of deaths in developing countries, according to the World Health Organization's *Burden of Disease* report.

Pollution has greater consequences:

⇨ Fisheries are destroyed.

⇨ Crops are damaged.

⇨ Production costs rise for industries that must filter dirty air or water to maintain product quality.

Extreme weather events (tornadoes, floods, hurricanes) are occurring more frequently and affecting more people than ever before. Poor people are the most vulnerable to environmental hazards.

As people move to cities from rural areas, environmental problems will increase. Rapid urbanisation – cities growing as people move from the countryside in search of better jobs and living conditions – often increases the burden for poor people living in slums.

What is the international community doing?

Environmental sustainability is a major global concern and is one of the United Nations Millennium Development Goals.

Many organisations are searching for ways to use natural resources so they last our lifetimes and remain available for generations to come.

International organisations like the World Bank work with developing countries to understand and address environmental challenges as countries continue to develop.

Countries and societies will make different choices about environmental priorities, but these choices need to be based on good analysis and the participation of all groups that will be affected by them.

Balancing and simultaneously achieving economic, social and environmental progress is difficult and often means difficult choices. Trade-offs among generations, social groups and countries influence what people see as sustainable development.

Concern for a sound global environment is an essential part of the World Bank's work to fight poverty. Environmental health – cleaning up the environment so that millions of people can live healthier lives – is especially important in this work.

The World Bank lends money to countries for environmental projects. It also requires environmental safeguards when lending money for development projects.

Some international initiatives concerned with the environment include:

⇨ Global Environment Facility (GEF) works on biodiversity conservation, climate change, ozone-depleting substances and international waters.

⇨ Multilateral Fund for the Implementation of the Montreal Protocol (MP) works to reverse the deterioration of the Earth's ozone layer.

⇨ Carbon Finance Business is working to create a global carbon market to reduce the emission of greenhouse gases as part of efforts to reduce climate change.

⇨ Critical Ecosystem Partnership Fund (CEPF) safeguards developing countries' biodiversity hotspots

⇨ World Bank/WWF Alliance for Forest Conservation and Sustainable Use aims to create and secure highly threatened protected areas, and certifies production forests as sustainable.

⇨ The above information is reprinted with kind permission from The World Bank. Visit www.youthink. worldbank.org for more information.

© 2011 The World Bank

REMIND ME AGAIN OF THE BENEFITS WE'LL ENJOY BY MOVING TO THE CITY?

Environmental justice

Information from Friends of the Earth.

What is environmental justice?

Environmental justice means everyone has:

⇨ a right to healthy places to live, work and enjoy themselves;

⇨ a right to a fair share of nature's benefits like food and water;

⇨ a responsibility to look after the planet for others and for future generations.

In doing this we not only ensure a better life for all of us – but help protect the environment too.

But to get environmental justice for everyone, society must change: we need a fairer world. This includes ordinary people having legal support and the political clout to influence decisions affecting the environment where they live.

In this article we highlight examples of environmental injustice – and describe what we're doing to tackle them. Read on and find out how we can work together for a fairer – and greener – future.

Environmental injustice around the world

Friends of the Earth believes that tackling environmental injustice will not only protect people, but also the natural world. If you have healthy people, you get a healthy planet. But to do this we have to get to grips with some big problems.

Inequality

People living in deprived areas have less influence on what happens to their environment – be it the site for a new factory or saving a forest from the chainsaws.

It's also people on the lowest incomes, who don't consume much, that cause the least environmental damage.

Yet poorer people are often worst hit when the environment is damaged. For example, the populations of developing countries are more likely to have their lives turned upside down by climate change. Already some low-lying Pacific islands are being abandoned because of rising seas.

Those with less money also get least out of what the planet has to offer us. The rich countries in the European Union have just seven per cent of the world's population. Yet they gobble up nearly a sixth of its resources – things like timber and metals for industry.

Transport

It's the less wealthy who are affected most by traffic. They get the health and congestion problems because they tend to live nearer big roads. Children in the UK's most deprived areas are five times more likely to be killed by traffic than those in richer areas.

The truth about offsetting... is it lets rich countries continue pumping out climate change gases while poorer countries are expected to develop cleanly

---

Fuel poverty

Four million UK households are in fuel poverty. This means they spend more than a tenth of their income on staying warm.

Poor laws

It's hard for people to use laws to protect their environment. For example, it's expensive for an individual to take a polluting company to court.

In the UK some planning laws are stacked against ordinary people. This means it's hard to have a say in decisions affecting where you live. Take the plans for a nuclear power station in Hartlepool. Locals were only given a few days' notice of when they would be consulted; many were not even aware the consultation was happening.

False climate solutions

Have you ever booked a holiday then paid to offset the emissions of your flight? Offsetting claims to help tackle

FRIENDS OF THE EARTH

climate change. For every tonne of carbon dioxide produced, the thinking goes, a tonne is avoided by investing in low-carbon projects.

The truth about offsetting, though, is it lets rich countries continue pumping out climate change gases while poorer countries are expected to develop cleanly. If we are to avoid catastrophic climate change, we need emissions cuts all round.

How we tackle environmental injustice

Friends of the Earth wants to solve problems, not complain about them. Our campaigns have brought about important changes, such as a world-leading climate change law. Here are some of the ways we want to tackle environmental injustice.

Solution – towards climate justice

At the heart of climate justice is a simple idea: those most responsible for climate change should be doing the most to tackle it.

Rich countries have benefited most from polluting the atmosphere – they've been pumping out climate-changing gases since Victorian times. Yet the world's poorest people are hit the hardest by global warming.

Poor countries are also less able to deal with the effects of climate change such as drought and severe flooding. Friends of the Earth is therefore campaigning for rich countries to:

⇨ take the lead on cutting carbon emissions and to do this now;

⇨ cut carbon by making real changes at home – not by offsetting emissions abroad, which will not tackle climate change;

⇨ pay for poorer countries to adapt to the effects of climate change;

⇨ help developing countries develop their own economies using clean technology, such as renewable energy.

Solution – better UK planning

Friends of the Earth is campaigning for planning laws that:

⇨ listen properly to the views of people who live locally;

⇨ give people and the environment as much importance as economic growth;

⇨ promote low-carbon solutions such as renewable energy.

In Merthyr Tydfil, South Wales, for example, there are plans to build a waste incinerator that would be the biggest in the UK. The community already has the largest UK open-cast coalmine on its doorstep. Friends of the Earth is working with the people of Merthyr to ensure they have a say in this big new decision for their community.

Solution – law in your hands

Friends of the Earth lawyers help people stand up for their rights. In 2008 we worked with a resident of Port Talbot, South Wales. He had obtained information showing pollution around a nearby steelworks broke legal levels. The lawyers worked with him to force the Welsh Assembly Government to produce plans to bring the pollution back within legal limits.

We're also working with people around the world to prevent destruction of rainforests and poisoning from pesticides.

Solution – Power Up

Every year Friends of the Earth runs a unique training weekend called Power Up. This helps people understand the planning system and their legal right to influence decisions affecting their communities.

Solution – fixing public transport

We are calling for every council to do its bit to tackle climate change. Part of this is pushing for better public transport that everyone can afford to use. Did you know that between 1997 and 2008 the real cost of motoring fell by 13 per cent? At the same time, bus and coach fares increased by 17 per cent, and rail fares by seven per cent.

July 2010

⇨ The above information is reprinted with kind permission from Friends of the Earth (England, Wales & N. Ireland). Visit www.foe.org for more information.

FRIENDS OF THE EARTH

Sustainability

Information from Population Matters.

Living sustainably means balancing our consumption, our technology choices and our population numbers in order to live within the resources of the planet. It means maintaining a stable and healthy environment for both humanity and biodiversity.

The implications are radical. As a minimum, a sustainable society, i.e. one that could physically be sustained indefinitely, would need a stable or reducing population, very high levels of reuse and recycling, 100% renewable energy and no net loss of soil and biodiversity. No country is yet near it.

We are already eating into our capital, collectively consuming the renewable resources of 1.5 planets.

There are no magic numbers, only trade-offs. Any given area of land can sustain many more very low-consuming poor people at bare subsistence than it can very high-consuming rich people living like millionaires. Better technology always helps; but basically, the richer we all become, the fewer of us the planet, or any country in it, can sustain; and the more of us there are, the lower our sustainable standard of living will be.

The choice is fewer who are richer, or more who are poorer.

Population Matters seeks an optimal balance, offering the best quality of life, not the greatest quantity of possessions. This implies modest but reasonably comfortable standards of living free from hunger or insecurity, which enables fulfilment without increasing physical consumption. Only non-physical things – like quality of relationships, intelligence, education, knowledge, skills, health, arts, spiritual growth, respect, fun – can increase indefinitely in a physically finite world.

Sustainable business and governmental policies would ensure the take-up of renewable energy and material sources while phasing out those with adverse side effects. Increased effort is needed to minimise waste of energy, water, food and other commodities. In a finite world even renewable resources are only available in limited quantities.

Halting population growth, and in many countries reversing it, is a vital part of living sustainably. In some societies, population growth has already slowed or stopped. Typically, the empowerment of women and improved availability of contraception have played major roles.

Compared with the challenge of asking people to reduce their living standards or change the fundamental technological basis of their society, approaches seeking a reduced birth rate are low cost and proven. The unborn people who never existed, and all their non-existent descendants in perpetuity, have no impact on our planet.

Gradually reducing our numbers back to the levels of one or two generations ago is one of the best ways of addressing the environmental and resource challenges we face.

Simple example

Take a simple example; a community has an aquifer of fossil groundwater, like a large water tank. The weather is reliable where they live and 100 m^3 of rainwater are added every day. To live sustainably, the community can use up to 100 m^3 of this water a day. If they use more one day they have to use less the next. The fact that the tank/aquifer is large and was full when they began beguiles some members of the community into believing they can use more. But their leaders resist; simple maths tells them that however large the tank/aquifer they cannot take out more than is put in, otherwise the tank/aquifer will eventually become empty. Yet in huge areas of the world, notably China, South Asia and even the USA, groundwater for irrigation and households is depleting daily. One day the pumps will run dry and stop.

⇨ The above information is reprinted with kind permission from Population Matters. Visit http://populationmatters.org for more information.

© Population Matters

POPULATION MATTERS

Sustainability and the city

An extract from SEPAView, the magazine by the Scottish Environment Protection Agency.

We need towns and cities. Most of us live in them, most of us work in them and they are our centres of culture, education and recreation. But towns and cities have needs: for space – resulting in the ever expansion of urban areas – for energy, water and food (usually transported over many miles) and for quality shared infrastructure and services. All those needs have consequences for the environment. With 50% of the UK's carbon dioxide emissions coming from the use of buildings and the emissions from construction and transport taken into account, towns and cities make a major contribution to climate change. Is it possible, then, for cities to be sustainable, and can they play a part in combating climate change?

Creating sustainable places

Creating sustainable places is part of how we can tackle climate change. One way to help achieve that is through the use of green infrastructure, which is a strategically planned network of green spaces and other environmental features in urban areas that support natural and ecological processes. Natural processes and solutions are increasingly being recognised as the preferred approach to tackling climate change, because green infrastructure provides a range of ecosystem services that make a substantial contribution towards adapting to our changing climate, and an important contribution towards mitigating the effects of climate change. Improving the natural value of a place also leads to the improvement of the health, happiness and prosperity of local communities.

Green infrastructure can contribute to climate change adaptation in many ways, particularly in managing temperature, water resources, surface water, flooding and habitat networks. UK climate projections predict increasing summer temperatures and higher incidences of extreme weather such as heatwaves. Urban environments also experience the 'heat island' effect, where they are warmer than the surrounding countryside.

Increased temperatures in urban areas increase the impact of air pollution, which if not properly managed can lead to damaged health. Open spaces can help reduce the effects of high temperatures by allowing air to circulate and have a cooling effect. Trees, especially those with large canopies, create shade, and water evaporating from trees and plants helps to cool air temperatures. Increasing all these elements, for example by creating more parks and introducing green roof systems, will help urban areas to remain comfortable places to live and work.

Working with water

Maintaining the quantity and quality of our water supply is essential. Sealed surfaces, such as roads and pavements, prevent water entering the ground and reaching aquifers and recharging groundwater. Trees, plants and green roofs provide soft ground that soaks up water and allows infiltration, and can also act as filters to remove pollutants.

Increasingly, during periods of heavy rainfall, water entering the sewer system is exceeding capacity. This is a result of the growing amount of sealed surfaces in towns and cities, which reduce natural drainage and increase the volume and speed of run-off. This can then lead to flooding. Surface water run-off can be reduced by introducing Sustainable Urban Drainage Systems (SUDS). SUDS mimic natural drainage, slowing and absorbing surface water. They can include green roofs, swales, wooded areas, ponds and wetlands.

The risk of flooding is increasing but the impact it has can be reduced. By working with natural processes, green infrastructure can contribute to an effective flood management strategy. This can include the creation of vegetated land which allows water to be absorbed into the ground or taken up by plants rather than entering the river system. Areas can also be identified that can be allowed to flood naturally without causing damage, such as the creation of urban wetlands. Wetland plants and vegetation alongside river banks also slow the flow of flood waters. Green infrastructure can help maintain existing, and create new, areas of habitat, bringing biodiversity into urban areas. It also plays an important role in creating habitat networks which connect fragmented habitats, allowing animals to migrate. This is particularly important for species that are vulnerable to the changing climate and have a limited ability to disperse. Wildlife corridors, which are areas of vegetation along roads, railways and rivers, can provide the connecting habitats that are needed to help species adapt to climate change.

⇨ The above information is reprinted with kind permission from Scottish Environment Protection Agency (SEPA). Visit www.sepa.org.uk for more information on this and other related topics.

© SEPA

SEPA

Resources and consumption

Resources and consumption campaign by Friends of the Earth Europe.

Europe is using an ever-increasing amount of the world's resources, and is now more dependent on imported resources than any other global region.

The Earth's ability to sustain this pattern of consumption is already being pushed to the limit. But Europe's dependence on imported resources also makes it economically vulnerable, with the extraction and processes of these resources having both social and environmental impacts.

Friends of the Earth Europe is calling on the EU to take the first steps to tackle this issue by ensuring that our resource use is measured, and by adopting new policies to increase our resource efficiency, such as higher recycling targets. We set out the case for this in our new briefing *Measuring Our Resource Use*.

The EU should also start to devise long-term targets and strategies in order to radically reduce our resource use.

Why is resource use important?

Natural resources are the foundation of our economy. Without the constant use of natural resources neither our economy nor our society could function. Nature provides humans with all the resources necessary for life, including:

⇨ energy for heat, electricity and mobility;

⇨ metals for high-tech equipment;

⇨ wood for furniture and paper products;

⇨ construction materials for our roads and houses;

⇨ food and water for a healthy diet.

As global standards of living increase, and the global population continues to rise, we are making ever-higher demands on the planet. This is creating competition between different regions of the world, with high resource prices impacting on the poor, and competition between different uses of resources: for example, whether land is used for food, fuels or biodiversity.

Resource use: a key sustainability issue

Our consumption of natural resources includes not just the physical materials that are extracted but also the global ecosystems, services and cycles that regulate conditions on the planet. Climate change is the first big environmental limit that humanity is facing: however, this is not the only ecological crisis being driven by our consumption of the Earth's resources. Others include:

⇨ the oceans are being emptied of fish far faster than they can replenish themselves;

⇨ forests are being cleared for animal feed and fuel crops such as soya and oil palm;

⇨ ecosystems and habitats are increasingly imperilled by pollution from industrial, extractive and dumping activity.

EU environmental policy – past, present and future

Over the past 30 years Europe has made significant progress in tackling environmental problems related to specific pollutants and harmful substances, such as air pollutants, sewage effluents and hazardous waste. But environmental problems related to the overall scale of European production and consumption are getting worse.

It is true that the EU has made significant progress in improving its resource efficiency: in other words, the amount of a product it can make for one euro, pound or dollar. However, this has not resulted in reduced consumption of natural resources by the EU, because these increases in efficiency have been outweighed by increases in consumption.

The current raft of EU environmental policies fail to adequately address the fundamental problem of rising resource use in a resource-finite world:

⇨ Despite years of discussion, the EU still doesn't measure its resource use, new polices are not assessed for their impact on resource use, and the EU has no targets to reduce our resource use.

⇨ Through its 'Raw Materials Initiative', the EU has shown more interest in securing access to resources from developing countries than in increasing Europe's resource efficiency. This focus jeopardises poverty alleviation and development in these countries.

⇨ Even in policy areas where the EU can easily achieve resource efficiency gains – such as waste policy – the EU is failing to bring in effective policy measures to make sure this happens. For example, a recent analysis for Friends of the Earth showed that Europe is currently burying and burning more than €5 billion of valuable resources.

FRIENDS OF THE EARTH

With the EU so dependent on imported resources, there is clearly an urgent need for more policies to boost eco-efficiency and reduce waste.

How can we measure Europe's resource use?

The EU does not currently measure its overall use of resources, which makes it difficult for targets to be set or policies to be evaluated.

Friends of the Earth Europe, together with the Sustainable Europe Research Institute (SERI) in Vienna, has been working to establish a set of effective but achievable indicators of resource use.

Following discussions with various experts, SERI have formulated a set of indicators, each of which includes the 'rucksack' of materials, land, water or greenhouse gas emissions that were used in making (or growing) a product:

⇨ Material use (which can also be divided into biotic and abiotic materials), including the rucksack of materials used in making imported products.

⇨ Total land use of countries (including via imported products), or the land use to make a product.

⇨ Water use of a country (including via imported products), or the water footprint of a product.

⇨ Greenhouse gas emissions (including emissions from imported products), or the carbon footprint of products.

All these indicators already exist, and they are all quite transparent, measuring clear physical quantities.

The indicators do not directly measure biodiversity impacts, though they can be used to highlight issues to be investigated – i.e. if a new policy (e.g. biofuel targets) results in a big increase in EU land use, then there should be further investigation.

They also don't address chemical or pollution issues, but indicators have not proved to be effective in this area, and specific regulation (e.g. the REACH chemicals policy) is more effective.

How would the measures be used?

⇨ The indicators can be used by the EU and governments to set targets, measure progress and establish policies (including in impact assessment of policy changes).

⇨ They can be used by companies to assess and improve the resource use associated with their products and activities.

Next steps

Friends of the Earth Europe wants to see these resource-use indicators adopted into the EU policy-making process. By doing so Europe will be taking the first steps to becoming not just a decarbonised but also a highly resource-efficient economy, with the social, environmental and economic benefits that would bring.

⇨ The above information is reprinted with kind permission from the non-governmental organisation (NGO), Friends of the Earth Europe. Visit www.foeeurope.org for more.

© Friends of the Earth Europe

FRIENDS OF THE EARTH

When it comes to the environment, education affects our actions

Findings from Understanding Society, the world's largest household panel survey, show that people with degrees are 25 per cent more likely on average than people with no academic qualifications to adopt pro-environmental behaviours, at least in terms of paying more for environmentally-friendly products.

The more highly-educated are more likely to display their environmental credentials through what they buy rather than with actions such as turning off lights, according to findings from Understanding Society, the world's largest household panel survey, funded by the Economic and Social Research Council (ESRC) and managed by the Institute of Social and Economic Research (ISER) at the University of Essex.

The first set of findings from the survey is based on data from more than 22,000 individuals and show that people with degrees are 25 per cent more likely, on average, than people with no academic qualifications to adopt pro-environmental behaviours, at least in terms of paying more for environmentally-friendly products. However, they are less likely to turn off the TV overnight or to use public transport.

Women are more likely than men to adopt pro-environmental behaviours

Overall, the survey, which will follow 40,000 UK households over many years, found that 60 per cent of people believed that a major environmental disaster is pending if things continue on their current course, and just over half the respondents (53 per cent) say they 'do quite a few things that are environmentally friendly' or are 'environmentally friendly in most things or everything' they do.

Nonetheless, people's willingness to behave in an environmentally-friendly way comes with conditions as 59 per cent of those surveyed agreed that 'any changes I make to help the environment need to fit in with my lifestyle' and just half (50 per cent) would be prepared to pay more for environmentally friendly products.

Professor Peter Lynn at the Institute of Social and Economic Research (ISER), which manages Understanding Society at the University of Essex, said: 'These findings offer an interesting suggestion that more highly-educated people may be more willing to take environmentally-motivated principled actions such as buying recycled paper products or avoiding the purchase of over-packaged products and yet are less willing than others to take relatively small actions that may be more of a personal inconvenience.'

The survey found that:

⇨ women are more likely than men to adopt pro-environmental behaviours: for example, they are four per cent more likely, on average, to be willing to pay more for environmentally-friendly products;

⇨ the presence of dependent children in the household is associated with a lower willingness to pay more for environmentally-friendly products;

⇨ employed people seem less likely to adopt pro-environmental behaviours – especially by putting on more clothes when cold and reducing the frequency of flights – than people who are outside the labour market.

Understanding Society also reveals that a significant minority have a defeatist attitude towards combating climate change. One in five (21 per cent) think that it is too late to do anything about climate change and nearly a third (29 per cent) believe it is not worth Britain trying to combat climate change, because other countries will just cancel out what we do.

Professor Lynn added: 'These initial findings suggest that people's behaviour is motivated by considerations other than environmental concern, such as income and personal resources. These motivations need to be better understood if policy makers and civil society organisations looking to change people's behaviours are to make any genuine headway. There clearly remains across all sections of society a considerable reluctance to take part in environmentally-friendly behaviour that has a personal cost, even though the importance of doing so is recognised by the majority of people.'

21 March 2011

⇨ The above information is reprinted with kind permission from the Economic and Social Research Council. Visit www.esrc.ac.uk for more information on this and other related topics.

© ESRC

ECONOMIC AND SOCIAL RESEARCH COUNCIL

Environmentalism, energy and consumer choice

Information from the Science Museum.

Although protestors are the most visible face of modern environmentalism, every member of society wields influence through the consumer choices they make. Collectively, consumers are powerful. The public can vote with their wallets by, for example, choosing organic vegetables or taking the bus instead of the car. Their actions will impact upon the companies that supply those commodities and the governments in charge of environmental strategy.

But consumer choices are not always easy to make. 'Green' alternatives are often more expensive than their unsustainable counterparts, while it is often hard to define which product or technology is more environmentally friendly than another.

The vast majority of the energy we consume is provided by fossil fuels (coal, oil and gas) and nuclear power. However, this approach is increasingly unsustainable

This complexity can be very clearly seen in the case of energy.

The vast majority of the energy we consume is provided by fossil fuels (coal, oil and gas) and nuclear power. However, this approach is increasingly unsustainable.

Reserves of fossil fuels are being exhausted and global warming, caused by carbon dioxide emissions, is beginning to impact on our everyday lives. Nuclear power is a sustainable energy source and does not produce carbon dioxide, but it raises a number of different security issues. It has a history of serious accidents, while nuclear waste can be a target for terrorism. Furthermore, a failsafe method of storing the waste without risking environmental contamination has not yet been found.

The solution to these problems is to develop renewable energy – energy that can be used without depleting its reserves. Sources include the sun (solar power), wind, waves and tides, biomass (plant and animals waste) and hydroelectric schemes.

But although these technologies are sustainable, they can be expensive or ineffective and they too can cause harm to the environment.

For example, there are many objections to tidal power schemes. The infrastructure they use can change currents and tides, destroying habitats and harming ocean ecosystems. Innovators are developing creative solutions to these problems.

Wind energy has the potential to play an important role in a more sustainable economy. It does not produce any pollutants and its source, the wind, will never run out. But various problems need to be resolved if it is to be exploited to its full potential.

Good positions for wind farms are often sites of great natural beauty so their construction is often opposed by conservationists. The turbines can occasionally be noisy, and can disrupt radio and TV signals with electro-magnetic interference. Wind farms have also led to the death of birds, although new turbine designs are eradicating that possibility.

Wind farms are also a relatively weak source of power. The amounts of energy that would be produced by even the most ambitious of planned wind farms are tiny compared with available nuclear power capacity.

So for all their advantages, current renewable energy solutions are not perfect. There will always be a price to pay, whether it comes in the form of higher heating bills, noisy wind farms on a once beautiful hillside, or increasing stockpiles of radioactive waste. Consumers can influence the evolution of energy policy and provision through the choices they make.

⇨ The above information is reprinted with kind permission from the Science Museum. Visit www.makingthemodernworld.org.uk for more information.

Waste and recycling: a quick guide

You can recycle a wide range of rubbish, from paper and glass to batteries, televisions and clothes. This saves energy and raw materials, and reduces the amount of waste sent to landfill sites. You can also help to reduce waste at home by composting and by repairing and reusing items.

The waste hierarchy

There are many ways of disposing of waste. The waste hierarchy lists these methods in a sliding scale, from the most environmentally-friendly option to the least for many types of waste:

1 Prevention – the best option, this focuses on reducing waste being produced in the first place.

2 Reuse – for example, using old food containers as lunch boxes or old plastic bags as bin liners.

3 Recycle – taking materials from old products to make something new, like making car parts from old metal drinks cans.

4 Energy recovery – creating energy from waste, for example by burning it to produce electricity.

5 Disposal – the worst option for most types of waste as this often involves burying rubbish in landfill.

Reduce waste

Recycling can help save materials and energy. It's even better to reduce the amount of things that are wasted in the first place.

The best way of doing this is simply using less. Try asking yourself if you need a product before buying it, and taking your own bags when you go shopping.

You can also be careful about what you buy. Choose items that will last longer and try to buy products you can use again instead of disposable items.

Reuse and repair

Repairing or reusing items means that they will last longer and won't need replacing with new items so quickly.

Even when you have finished with something, someone else will often be able to use it. Second-hand furniture, clothes and electrical items like mobiles are especially popular: why not pass them onto friends and family? You could also sell them, donate them to charity or pass them on via sharing schemes.

Try looking for items you want from auction sites or giveaway sites like Freecycle or Freegle. You may even bag yourself a bargain.

Recycle

Paper, glass, plastic bottles, garden waste, fridges, shoes, batteries – all of these and more can be recycled, helping to save energy and new materials.

Most councils run recycling collections from your doorstep, while waste and recycling centres (the local tip) can also accept many other materials for recycling.

An average family can double or even treble the amount they recycle.

What can be recycled

Most councils run doorstep collections for materials such as paper, glass, plastics and cardboard. Local civic amenity sites (your local tip) can also accept many other materials for recycling.

Everything can be recycled, from wood, shoes, textiles and TVs, to electrical equipment, light bulbs, fridges and freezers. Even small items of furniture can sometimes be recycled.

Check with your local council to see what can be recycled in your area.

Buy recycled products

Products made from recycled goods save raw materials and increase the demand for recycled materials. You can buy recycled household goods and fashion items like shoulder bags, plastic trays, pencil cases and aluminium foil.

Compost your garden and food waste

Around a third of all household waste collected by local authorities is organic waste (garden and food) which could be composted.

If organic waste is sent to landfill, it produces methane, which has strong climate change effects. Composting waste like teabags, vegetable peelings, shredded paper and egg boxes reduces these climate change effects and saves valuable space in landfill sites.

It's easy to make compost, and it provides a rich and natural source of nourishment for your garden. Many councils provide compost bins at a reduced rate, so

contact your local council to find out what is available in your area.

Dispose of hazardous waste items safely

Some items contain hazardous materials and need to be carefully disposed of to avoid environmental problems like water pollution. Examples of things that need to be disposed of at a proper facility include: paint, batteries, electrical equipment and oil.

Electrical equipment and batteries can all be recycled and the precious resources used to make new items.

⇨ Information from Directgov. Visit www.direct.gov.uk for more information.

© Crown copyright

Waste and recycling

The UK consumes natural resources at an unsustainable rate and contributes unnecessarily to climate change. Each year we generate over 80 million tonnes of waste, which causes environmental damage and costs businesses and consumers money.

The Government has published the findings of its review of waste policy, setting out its policies and a series of actions designed to help move towards a zero waste economy in England. Alongside the review, the Government also published an *Anaerobic Digestion Strategy and Action Plan*.

Key facts and figures

⇨ Around 40% of waste from households is currently recycled, as of 2011, compared to 11% in 2000/01.

⇨ The average residual waste per person has reduced by 76 kg since 2006/07 to 275 kg/person/year.

The UK produces approximately seven million (five in England) tonnes of food waste per year

⇨ 52% of commercial and industrial waste was recycled or reused in England in 2009, compared to 42% in 2002/03.

⇨ 55% of municipal waste generated in the UK is sent to landfill, compared to an EU-27 average of 40%.

⇨ According to RecycleNow, UK recycling saves more than 18 million tonnes of carbon dioxide a year – equivalent to taking five million cars off the road.

⇨ The UK produces approximately seven million (five in England) tonnes of food waste per year and about 90 million (40-60 in England) tonnes of animal slurry and manure that could realistically be available for utilisation by anaerobic digestion (AD) technology.

55% of municipal waste generated in the UK is sent to landfill, compared to an EU-27 average of 40%

⇨ In England this could generate at least 3-5 TWh (terrawatt hours) electricity per year by 2020 (a heat equivalent of 6-10 TWh).

⇨ The UK water industry treats 66% of sewage sludge by AD, generating in the region of 1 TWh per year of electricity in 2010.

⇨ The diversion of biodegradable wastes to AD can reduce greenhouse gas emissions from landfill. For example, capturing the biogas from one tonne of food waste will save between a half and one tonne of CO_2 equivalent.

⇨ Direct emissions from the waste management greenhouse gas inventory sector in the UK accounted for 3.2% of the UK's total estimated emissions of greenhouse gases in 2009, or 17.9 Mt CO_2e compared to 59 Mt CO_2e in 1990. Of the 2008 total, 89% arises from landfill, 10% from waste-water handling and 2% from waste incineration (these figures are rounded).

⇨ The above information is reprinted with kind permission from the Department for Environment, Food and Rural Affairs. Visit www.defra.gov.uk for more.

© Crown copyright

Western lifestyles plundering tropics at record rate, WWF report shows

Living Planet *report shows planet's resources are being used at 1.5 times the rate nature can replace them – but long-term decline of animal life appears to have been halted.*

By Juliette Jowit

The Earth's population is using the equivalent of 1.5 planets' worth of natural resources, but the long-term decline of animal life appears to have been halted, a WWF report shows.

The latest *Living Planet* report, published today by the conservation group, also reveals the extent to which modern Western lifestyles are plundering natural resources from the tropics at record levels.

The report shows the impact of living off the planet's 'savings': in the last 40 years human consumption has doubled, while the Living Planet index – measuring the decline and increase of thousands of species on land, in rivers and at sea – has declined by 30% overall, and by a massive 60% in the tropics.

However, the index – compiled by the Zoological Society of London (ZSL) and likened to a stock market charting the progress of the natural world – shows that animal populations have risen significantly in the richer nations in the temperate zones north and south of the tropics, and globally appear to have stabilised in the last few years.

Despite the suggestion of good news, WWF and supporters at the launch warned that there were still severe threats, especially from climate change and water shortages.

'Healthy ecosystems form the basis of all we have – lose them and we destroy our life-support system,' said Jonathan Baillie, ZSL's conservation programme director.

'This is like spending the savings: we're spending the natural capital we have on this planet,' said Jim Leape, WWF's director, at the launch of the report in Bristol. 'That's an economic crisis in the making.'

> **'Healthy ecosystems form the basis of all we have – lose them and we destroy our life-support system'**

Measurements of the 'ecological footprint' of different countries – the area required to provide the resources consumed by the population or average person in a year, compiled by the Global Footprint Network – shows the richest countries consume, on average, five times the quantity of natural resources of the poorest countries. At the extremes are the United Arab Emirates, with an average footprint of more than ten hectares, and Timor-Leste at less than one hectare. The global average is about three hectares, and the UK figure is around five.

'There's going to be global trade and that's not always a bad thing,' said Colin Butfield, head of campaigns for WWF. '[But people] in many subsistence countries depend on their local water source and if upstream you have got a big industrial cotton- or soy-growing plant, we're starting to affect in many, many cases around the world the ability for poor people to develop, feed themselves, industrialise, to supply basic products we use every day: soy beans for cattle, cotton for clothing, and so on.

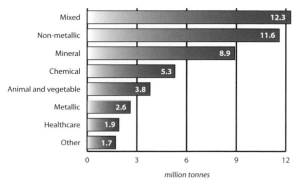

Commercial and industrial waste management (in million tonnes), 2009

Recycled	Landfill	Re-used	Other
23.6	11.3	1.3	11.7

(*million tonnes*)

Commercial and industrial waste by type (in million tonnes), 2009

Type	million tonnes
Mixed	12.3
Non-metallic	11.6
Mineral	8.9
Chemical	5.3
Animal and vegetable	3.8
Metallic	2.6
Healthcare	1.9
Other	1.7

Source: Government review of waste policy in England 2011, Department for Environment, Food and Rural Affairs, © Crown copyright

THE GUARDIAN

'We're also taking away the natural capital of those countries, and only a small number of people in those countries benefit.'

The latest index compiled the results for nearly 8,000 populations of more than 2,500 different species of mammals, reptiles, amphibians, birds and fish. The real picture is, however, likely to be worse, because the latest report includes new populations, and because there are still many tropical species which have not been identified by scientists yet, said Butfield. It also does not directly measure the fate of plants, or pollution.

The Earth's population is using the equivalent of 1.5 planets' worth of natural resources

Nick Ross, the TV presenter, who joined the launch event, called it 'a bonfire of biodiversity'.

'The trajectory is so alarming that even if people pick little holes in the methodology, the message that comes across here is overwhelming,' he said.

The report says the biggest impact on the global footprint of humanity is an 11-fold increase in carbon emissions in the last four decades. In another 40 years the footprint would double again, forecasted Leape.

There also needed to be more support to sustainable alternatives to modern consumption, such as timber, fish, soy and other commodities from well-managed sources, said WWF

The report, which is published just weeks before a major conference on slowing or halting the loss of biodiversity in Nagoya, Japan, calls for a series of changes to help address the problems, including more protected areas, zero net deforestation, eliminating over-fishing and destructive fishing practices, and finding ways to put a value on biodiversity and ecosystem services.

There also needed to be more support for sustainable alternatives to modern consumption, such as timber, fish, soy and other commodities from well-managed sources, said WWF. Although government regulation was the 'ideal' way to achieve this, consumers and businesses also needed to insist on such standards, said Butfield. 'The reality of politics is government will only move a certain amount of the way, depending on how much they think consumers and businesses are behind them,' he said.

13 October 2010

© Guardian News and Media Limited 2010

Energy security is a top concern for Brits

Energy security is the leading environmental issue for Britons, over and above climate change, according to a new international Ipsos poll of working-age adults.

Half of Britons (50%) feel that future energy supplies and sources are one of the most important environmental issues facing the nation. Other leading issues are waste management (48%); overpopulation (41%), and global warming/climate change (25%).

Of the 24 nations polled across the globe, Britain is in the bottom third in terms of concern around climate change. Lower-placed nations include South Africa (23%), China (21%), Poland (19%) and Russia (9%). In contrast, we are in the top three nations most concerned about energy security, behind Sweden (58%) and Germany (56%).

Ipsos MORI's Head of Environment Research, Edward Langley, said:

'The public are cautious about climate change. They feel there is a lack of consensus on whether it is man-made and the degree to which it will impact their lives. In contrast, our dependency on fossil fuels is a more immediate and tangible risk that they can get their heads around, and one where they see an obvious need to take action to maintain living standards.'

There are a number of potential implications for environmental campaigners. Firstly, it is important for the public to realise that the science community is in broad agreement that man-made climate change is happening, and to link the impacts with risks the public care about: that is, our economic prosperity and that of our children. Secondly, campaigners need to consider the degree to which energy security can be used as a hook to encourage participation in sustainable behaviours.

Looking further afield, campaigners may also consider why other nationalities are more likely to feel climate change is a key environmental issue. For example, Japan (48%), Canada (40%), Spain (40%) and Germany (38%) are much more likely to say climate change is a key issue for them. Are there lessons which can be learnt in terms of how the public have been engaged there?

⇨ Information from Ipsos MORI. Visit www.ipsos-mori.com for more information.

© Ipsos MORI

Scandal of UK's illegal e-waste trade exposed

A toxic flood of discarded technology is illegally leaving the UK to wash up in Africa, the Environmental Investigation Agency (EIA) reveals in its new report System Failure: The UK's harmful trade in electronic waste.

Disposing of e-waste is fast becoming big business and EIA's 18-month undercover operation – the most thorough to date into the illegal underbelly of the trade – shows that the chance to make a quick buck at the expense of the developing world is too tempting for some to resist.

E-waste most commonly comprises everyday electrical goods such as mobile phones, televisions, stereos, laptops, PCs and printers. European Union regulations require it to be properly recycled, either here or in other developed countries.

But EIA investigators probing the illegal export of waste cathode ray tubes (CRTs) have uncovered a highly lucrative international e-waste black market involving many players at every level, from small-time electronic brokers to large organisations, local councils and even major central government institutions.

NOW WE CAN ALL EXPERIENCE THE COMPUTER AGE...

Illegally shipped out in bulk to developing countries, the waste is stripped down to bare components by primitive methods: copper wires are bundled and set alight to remove flame-resistant coatings, emitting vast quantities of toxic dioxins; CRT monitors are smashed with hammers, releasing plumes of lead dust.

Poverty drives young children to carry out this work to help support their families, and the potential health consequences for them are dire – reproductive and developmental problems, damaged immune, nervous and blood systems, kidney damage and impaired brain development in the young.

The UK appears to be an especially large contributor to the problem, with the majority of its illegal shipments arriving in Nigeria and Ghana, despite ostensibly working under the scrutiny of companies approved by local government and Producer Compliance Schemes.

African countries need good quality second-hand electronic goods, but the high demand for items such as TVs, PCs and fridges is being exploited by unscrupulous traders and 'waste tourists', Africans who travel to the UK to buy used electronic goods from brokers – when their shipment arrives in African ports it often comprises about 75 per cent waste but the profits to be made from the working goods are enough to make it viable.

In 2009, EIA investigators set out to infiltrate smuggling networks by established a front company to enable trade negotiations with a number of firms involved in exporting and trading in e-waste.

Investigators learned how traders frequently circumvent customs checks by mislabelling waste CRTs as working, using generic terms such as 'personal effects' or 'used household goods' on shipping documents and adopting a 'no-questions-asked' approach, knowingly offering untested CRTs for export and so shirking their responsibility of due care.

EIA was offered untested CRTs by brokers who claimed to have contracts with various government institutions, including the Ministry of Defence, the Fire Service and the NHS.

In Spring 2010, undercover investigators visited six civic amenity sites in Greater London to look for signs

ENVIRONMENTAL INVESTIGATION AGENCY

of e-waste leakage. At council recycling centres in Croydon and Merton, they were shown how workers separated higher-quality TVs from others being dumped. Investigators were told the sets are purchased by another company, Sanak Ventures UK Ltd of London, which claims to refurbish them for export.

To check that only working TVs were being exported, EIA hid trackers inside TVs which were deliberately disabled beyond repair and left at the council sites. Several weeks later, one appeared in Nigeria and the other in Ghana, clearly showing neither had been tested prior to export.

Electronic waste collection at both civic amenity sites is run by Environmental Waste Controls, one of the UK's largest waste and recycling management companies with numerous high-profile clients including Morrisons, Tesco, Asda, Barclays, Hilton, MBNA and Prudential, the NHS and Network Rail. EIA's investigations indicate that similar practices may be the norm in almost 50 other council recycling sites run by the company, located in Blackburn, Leicester, Loughborough, north Wales, west London and Yorkshire.

EIA has also drawn attention to the systematic failure of Producer Compliance Schemes in facilitating illegal trade. Information on contract rates paid to recyclers suggests that competition between the UK's 36 Producer Compliance Schemes is so fierce that rates paid to recyclers are well below the minimum costs of recycling.

'EIA's work clearly demonstrates the UK's failure to take its environmental responsibility seriously,' said Fin Walravens, EIA Senior Campaigner. 'Our e-waste isn't a new problem and it isn't going away. It's time for the Government and enforcement agencies to give this issue the resources and attention it warrants.'

Urgent call to action from Environmental Investigation Agency

⇨ The Government should:

↳ ensure continued funding for the Environment Agency to develop its intelligence-led enforcement approach;

↳ conduct a full review of the Producer Compliance Scheme system;

↳ commission a review of existing contracts between local authorities and Producer Compliance Schemes to ensure they have the means to carry out recycling, including scrutiny of sub-contracts between compliance schemes and service operators.

⇨ The awarding of Producer Compliance Scheme contracts should be taken off local authorities and centralised in the relevant government ministry.

⇨ All e-waste left at Designated Collection Facilities must be quantified, and audited records kept.

⇨ Producer Compliance Schemes holding the contract for sites from which e-waste has been illegally exported should lose their contract after successful prosecution.

⇨ The Environment Agency should tighten its procedures for licensing authorised treatment facilities and contractors, including increased spotchecks.

16 May 2011

↳ The above information is reprinted with kind permission from the Environmental Investigation Agency. Visit www.eia-international.org for more information.

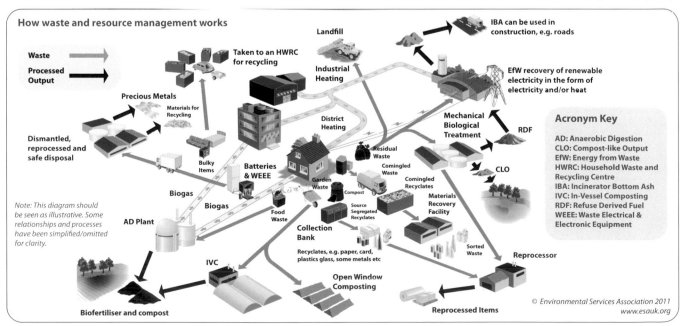

How waste and resource management works

Note: This diagram should be seen as illustrative. Some relationships and processes have been simplified/omitted for clarity.

Acronym Key

AD: Anaerobic Digestion
CLO: Compost-like Output
EfW: Energy from Waste
HWRC: Household Waste and Recycling Centre
IBA: Incinerator Bottom Ash
IVC: In-Vessel Composting
RDF: Refuse Derived Fuel
WEEE: Waste Electrical & Electronic Equipment

© *Environmental Services Association 2011*
www.esauk.org

ENVIRONMENTAL INVESTIGATION AGENCY

Attitudes of Europeans towards the issue of biodiversity

An extract from the main findings of a report by the European Commission.

Biodiversity threats

⇨ When asked about the most important threats to biodiversity, more than a quarter of EU citizens (27%) mentioned air and water pollution. A similar proportion (26%) mentioned man-made disasters, such as oil spills or industrial accidents.

⇨ Roughly a fifth (19%) of respondents selected intensive farming, deforestation and over-fishing, 13% chose climate change and 9% mentioned the creation of more roads, houses or industrial sites, and changes in land use as the most important threat to biodiversity.

⇨ The proportion of respondents who selected water and air pollution as the main threats to biodiversity ranged from 15% in Belgium to 39% in Poland and Romania. Similarly, the proportion who mentioned man-made disasters (such as oil spills or industrial accidents) was just 13%-14% in Finland, Ireland and the UK, but reached 51% in Cyprus.

⇨ The combination of intensive farming, deforestation and over-fishing was selected as the most important threat to biodiversity by more than a quarter of respondents in the Netherlands (31%), the UK (29%) and Germany (26%).

Biodiversity loss: seriousness of the problem

⇨ More than eight in ten EU citizens (84%-93%) felt that biodiversity loss was a very or fairly serious problem at national, European and global levels.

⇨ Comparing the results of 2007 and 2010, it was noted that respondents in the current survey were somewhat less likely to think that biodiversity loss was a serious problem in their country. The overall proportion of respondents who thought that biodiversity loss was a serious global problem, however, was unchanged in the two surveys.

⇨ Individual results in Member States showed large variations in citizens' perceptions regarding the seriousness of biodiversity loss in their own country. The proportion of respondents who said that biodiversity loss was a very serious domestic problem ranged from 9% in Finland to 72% in Portugal (together with 57%-60% in Italy, Greece and Romania).

⇨ Similarly, a majority of respondents in Portugal (75%), Italy (62%), Cyprus (55%), Greece and Romania (both 52%) reported that biodiversity loss was a very serious problem in Europe.

⇨ The proportions of respondents who considered biodiversity loss to be a very serious global problem ranged from 46% in Estonia to 82% in Portugal. Across almost all countries, not more than one in 20 respondents doubted whether biodiversity loss was a serious global problem.

⇨ In terms of being affected by biodiversity loss, most EU citizens saw no immediate personal impact. A sixth of respondents (17%) said they had already been affected by biodiversity loss, compared to almost three-quarters (72%) who thought that it would only have an impact in the future.

⇨ Portuguese respondents stood out from the pack with a slim majority (54%) who said they were already being personally affected by the extinction of flora and fauna and roughly a fifth (22%) who foresaw themselves being affected by biodiversity loss in the near future.

⇨ A comparison of the 2007 and 2010 results showed not much change in most countries in the proportion of respondents who doubted if biodiversity loss would have any effect at all.

March 2010

⇨ Source: *Attitude of Europeans towards the issue of biodiversity*

EUROPEAN UNION

Biodiversity loss degrades natural capital and ecosystem services

Information from the European Environment Agency.

Biodiversity includes all living organisms found in the atmosphere, on land and in water. All species have a role and provide the 'fabric of life' on which we depend: from the smallest bacteria in the soil to the largest mammal in the ocean. The four basic building blocks of biodiversity are genes, species, habitats and ecosystems. The preservation of biodiversity is fundamental to human wellbeing and sustainable provisioning of natural resources. Furthermore, it is closely intertwined with other environmental issues, such as adaptation to climate change or protecting human health.

Europe's biodiversity is heavily influenced by human activities including agriculture, forestry and fisheries, as well as urbanisation. Roughly half of Europe's land area is farmed, most forests are exploited, and natural areas are increasingly fragmented by urban areas and infrastructural development. The marine environment is also heavily affected, not just by unsustainable fisheries, but also by other activities such as offshore extraction of oil and gas, sand and gravel extraction, shipping, and offshore wind farms.

The preservation of biodiversity is fundamental to human wellbeing and sustainable provisioning of natural resources

Exploitation of natural resources typically leads to disturbance and changes in the diversity of species and habitats. Conversely, extensive agricultural patterns, as seen in Europe's traditional agricultural landscapes, have contributed to a higher species diversity at a regional level if compared to what could be expected in strictly natural systems. Over-exploitation, however, can lead to degradation of natural ecosystems and ultimately to species extinctions. Examples of such ecological feedbacks are the collapse of commercial fish stocks through overfishing, the decline of pollinators due to intensive agriculture, and reduced water retention and increased flooding risks due to the destruction of moorland.

By introducing the concept of ecosystem services, the Millennium Ecosystem Assessment turned the debate on biodiversity loss upside down. Beyond conservationist concerns, biodiversity loss has become an essential part of the debate on human wellbeing and the sustainability of our lifestyle, including consumption patterns.

Loss of biodiversity can thus lead to degradation of 'ecosystem services' and undermine human wellbeing.

Over-exploitation, however, can lead to degradation of natural ecosystems

Evidence is growing that ecosystem services are under great pressure globally due to the over-exploitation of natural resources in combination with human-induced climate change. Ecosystem services are often taken for granted, but are in fact very vulnerable. The soil, for example, is a key component of ecosystems, supports a rich variety of organisms and provides many regulating and supporting services. Yet it is only, at most, a few metres thick (and often considerably less), and subject to degradation through erosion, pollution, compaction and salinisation.

Although Europe's population is expected to remain roughly stable over the next decades, the consequences for biodiversity of increasing global resource demand for food, fibres, energy and water, and lifestyle changes are expected to continue to manifest themselves. Further land-cover conversion and intensification of land use, both in Europe and in the rest of the world, may negatively affect biodiversity – directly through, for example, habitat destruction and resource depletion, or indirectly through, for example, fragmentation, drainage, eutrophication, acidification and other forms of pollution.

Developments in Europe are likely to affect land-use patterns and biodiversity around the globe – demand for natural resources in Europe already exceeds its own production. The challenge is therefore to reduce Europe's impact on the global environment while maintaining biodiversity at a level where ecosystem services, the sustainable use of natural resources and human wellbeing are secured.

⇨ The above information is reprinted with kind permission from the European Environment Agency. Visit www.eea.europa.eu for more information.

© *European Environment Agency*

A history of climate change

Tackling climate change is one of the biggest challenges this generation faces, and the first step is to understand exactly what it is. Find out how climate change was first detected, the history of efforts to tackle it and the latest developments.

What is climate change?

The Earth's climate is not static. Over the billions of years of Earth's existence, it has changed many times in response to natural causes.

However, when people talk about 'climate change' today, they mean the changes in temperature over the last 100 years caused by human activity. During this time, the average temperature of the atmosphere near the Earth's surface has risen by about 0.75 degrees Celsius.

Nearly all climate scientists agree that global temperatures will rise further – by how much depends on future emissions of greenhouse gases, and other human activities.

If the temperature rise is high, the impact is likely to be extreme and it will be difficult to cope with. There are likely to be more intense and frequent extreme weather events – like heatwaves, floods and tropical storms – and sea levels will rise further.

The world's response to climate change

The first major international climate science conference was held in 1979. The conference called on governments 'to foresee and prevent potential man-made changes in climate'.

United Nations takes action

In 1988, the United Nations set up the Intergovernmental Panel on Climate Change (IPCC) to analyse and report on scientific findings. The IPCC warned that only strong measures to stop greenhouse gas emissions would prevent serious global warming.

Global targets for reducing emissions

In 1992, the Earth Summit took place in Rio de Janeiro. Here, the United Nations Framework Convention on Climate Change (UNFCCC) was signed by 154 nations. It agreed to prevent 'dangerous' warming from greenhouse gases and set voluntary targets for reducing emissions. The UK is one of a small number of countries which met this voluntary target.

Kyoto: legally binding cuts in emissions

In 1997, the Kyoto Protocol was agreed. Where the UNFCCC agreed voluntary targets, Kyoto was the first international treaty to set legally binding emissions cuts for industrialised nations. It was signed by 178 countries and came into force in 2005.

Latest international action on climate change

In 2007, the IPCC announced that the planet has warmed about 0.75 degrees Celsius since the beginning of the 20th century. It said there is a greater than 90 per cent chance that global warming over the last 50 years is due to human activity. At the 2007 UN climate change conference in Bali, the world's nations agreed to negotiate on a deal to tackle climate change.

At the United Nations (UN) conference in Cancun 2010 the attendees agreed a global deal to tackle climate change. The key parts of this agreement were:

⇨ an overall target limit of two degrees Celsius on temperature rise;

⇨ to include measures that developed and developing countries are taking on climate change in the UN agreement;

⇨ a system to assess how countries are living up to their promises on emissions;

⇨ the Green Climate Fund to help developing countries go low carbon;

⇨ to slow, halt and reverse the destruction of trees;

⇨ to set up ways to help developing countries access low carbon technologies.

What you can do about climate change

Some further changes to the Earth's climate are inevitable, but there is still time to have a positive influence on the future. You can help minimise further changes and adapt to those that will happen through your decisions and actions. Read about simple things you can do to make a difference in 'Greener living: a quick guide to what you can do', which can be found on the Directgov website.

⇨ Information from Directgov. Visit www.direct.gov.uk for more information.

DIRECTGOV

REDD herring

Will the UN's latest initiative to save rainforests really work? Simon Birch looks to environmental groups for an answer.

With the world's rainforests still going up in smoke at an ever-increasing rate, the good news is that a new global initiative is being billed as a way of helping. REDD (yes, it's another clumsy acronym: Reducing Emissions from Deforestation in Developing Countries) is now official UN policy in the fight against climate change.

The REDD proposals have come about as a consequence of the 2006 Stern Report, which identified that carbon dioxide emissions resulting from rainforest destruction account for a massive 20% of the world's total. The idea behind REDD is, in theory at least, quite simple: rich Northern countries will offset their own greenhouse gas emissions by paying poorer Southern countries not to level their rainforests. The whole scheme, which will cost billions of dollars, would then be paid for by the sale of carbon credits on the emerging global carbon market.

Divided movement

So much for the good news. The bad news is that the environmental movement is now becoming increasingly divided over the potential benefits of REDD and its ability to save any rainforest at all. Leading the REDD sceptics is forest campaigner Chris Lang from redd-monitor.org. 'Saving the rainforests was one of the biggest green issues in the '80s but somehow it's slipped off the agenda,' says Lang. 'The only positive thing about REDD is that people are now talking about rainforests again, beyond that the whole idea of REDD is just nonsensical.'

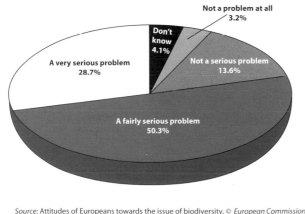

How serious is the decline and possible extinction of animal species, flora and fauna, natural habitats and ecosystems in your country?

Not a problem at all
3.2%

Don't know
4.1%

A very serious problem
28.7%

Not a serious problem
13.6%

A fairly serious problem
50.3%

Source: Attitudes of Europeans towards the issue of biodiversity, © European Commission

'For starters,' says Lang, 'the World Bank, countless aid agencies and campaign groups including Greenpeace have been trying to save rainforests for decades without any real success. The idea that by throwing vast sums of money at the problem you'll succeed where everyone else before has failed is frankly ridiculous.'

Lang goes on to point out that the majority of the world's remaining rainforests are found in some of the most corrupt and unstable countries in the world, most notably Laos and the Democratic Republic of Congo. 'It's just naïve to expect these countries to suddenly turn around and say "we've changed" when faced with the prospect of being given vast amounts of money to stop logging their rainforests. It just won't happen.'

Land grab?

Owen Espley from Friends Of the Earth shares Lang's scepticism. 'We're also concerned that the huge sums of money that are being talked about will lead to a massive land-grab from the world's 60 million indigenous rainforest people who depend upon the rainforests for their livelihoods.'

> ### The project... will be paid for by the sale of carbon credits

However, the chief concern of those environmental groups who are at best lukewarm about REDD is that it simply won't achieve its core objective, i.e. reducing global greenhouse gas emissions. 'Our worry is that REDD is entirely driven by the need for rich, industrial Northern countries to offset their greenhouse gas emissions and not take action at home to cut emissions – which won't solve anything,' says Cath Long from the Rainforest Foundation.

Meanwhile, Fauna and Flora International is one of the environmental groups which see REDD's potential in preserving rainforests and has been involved in establishing one of the world's first REDD projects.

Tigers saved

Nearly two million acres of rainforest in Sumatra, home to the rare Sumatran tiger, have now been protected. The project is expected to prevent 100 million tonnes of carbon dioxide emissions from being released into the atmosphere by slashing the rate of deforestation by up to 85%.

Backed by bankers

The project, now backed by international bankers Merrill

Lynch, will be paid for by the sale of carbon credits, the first of which are expected to go on sale this year. 'We're keen to tap into the world's financial markets to secure rainforest conservation,' says Annelisa Grigg from FFI. So does Grigg believe that the market is the answer to rainforest destruction?

'Absolutely not, as the drivers of deforestation are very complex. What the market offers is just one solution which needs to sit within a whole package of measures which must, for example, address the issue of corruption and governance,' replies Grigg – who then takes a swipe at those critics of REDD: 'REDD is a very new project so people are going to be a little bit scared by it.'

Uncertainty

Bryony Worthington, former climate campaigner at FoE and now the founder of the climate change action group sandbag.org.uk, remains unconvinced however: 'REDD won't end up saving rainforests simply because the global carbon market isn't yet mature enough to take that much uncertainty – which REDD will undoubtedly bring,' states Worthington.

What's more, Worthington believes that not only will REDD fail in its core objective, it's actually potentially dangerous: 'Our fear is that REDD will drive investment away from developing carbon-free technologies which we need right now if we're to avert climate change catastrophe.'

⇨ The above information is reprinted with kind permission from Ethical Consumer. Visit www.ethicalconsumer.org for more information.

© Ethical Consumer

Forgotten forests have vital role in keeping deserts at bay

Information from the Chartered Institution of Water and Environmental Management (CIWEM).

Dryland forests are in the vanguard of the battle to halt the spread of deserts in arid countries, maintaining the productivity of farmland and a sustainable way of life. They cover a fifth of the land area of arid zones, yet few people have heard of them, and fewer appreciate their value. That must change, says the Chartered Institution of Water and Environmental Management (CIWEM) on World Day to Combat Desertification.

Deforestation conjures up images of areas of tropical rainforest the size of small European counties or US states being cleared by commercial logging or ranching interests, or perhaps to make space for biofuel crop plantations. But in countries of the world where populations face abject poverty daily because of poor crop yield or failure, exacerbated by encroaching deserts, healthy forests are a lifeline.

In such arid and semi-arid zones, poverty and need for food and fuel can lead to dryland forests being cleared for farmland as well as for wood fuel to burn. Often these parts of the world, which constitute a third of the planet's land area and half that of developing countries, face the greatest pressures from development and population growth.

This forest loss leads to less food availability for browsing livestock as well as to loss of biodiversity. But the effect can be reversed and good farming practice and maintenance or replanting of forests can have dramatic and positive effects for farmers, providing shelter for crops, food for livestock, a sustainable supply of fuel and far fewer failed crop sowings.

The United Nations Convention to Combat Desertification has designated dryland forests as the focus for World Day to Combat Desertification 2011.

Forest loss leads to less food availability for browsing livestock as well as to loss of biodiversity

CIWEM's Executive Director, Nick Reeves, says:

'Without wishing to sound crass, dryland forests aren't glam. They don't have the soaring majesty of many tropical and some temperate forests, or the abundant biodiversity that rainforests support, but they are of vital importance to developing countries, particularly through the support systems they provide.

'Their benefits are often very immediately felt, but somehow they have been below the radar of the international community. There is a real need to spread good land management practices in dryland areas and to sell the benefits to communities of maintaining and improving their forests. It is important that the international community support these measures.'

⇨ The above information is reprinted with kind permission from CIWEM. Visit www.ciwem.org.uk for more information.

© CIWEM

The marine environment

Information from Defra.

Our seas offer millions of people a chance to enjoy the natural environment; provide healthy, secure food supplies and other resources; and support employment in coastal communities. Healthy, productive, sustainable marine ecosystems contain rich and varied wildlife, plants and geological features. They provide a wide range of ecosystem services, including helping to mitigate the effects of climate change.

We subject our seas to competing demands, as well as pollution and other damage. They help to regulate our climate, but their ecosystems are threatened by warming and acidification. Some fish stocks are not fished at sustainable levels and some habitats and species are threatened by the pressures on our seas.

Marine issues are of global concern. The seas offer opportunities to take action on climate change through adaption and mitigation and the UK is taking a lead internationally on issues such as ocean acidification. We are also taking a lead to protect whales and prevent illegal fishing.

Our seas are a common public resource so the Government aims to ensure they are sustainably managed for a range of social, environmental and economic benefits. The UK has national, EU and international marine conservation commitments. Defra designates marine protected areas, which play a key part in achieving biodiversity benefits. We are also tackling the issues of how best to strike a balance between conservation and development of marine resources. Supplies of fish as a healthy food source need to be secured, without destroying fish stocks and damaging the marine environment.

Key facts and figures

⇨ Seas and oceans absorb 25% of global carbon emissions from human activity.

⇨ UK seas contain rich and varied wildlife, with over 8,000 species represented.

⇨ Seas provide revenue from oil and gas (£37 billion), maritime transport (£4.7 billion), leisure and recreation (£1.3 billion), coastal tourism (£5.3 billion), naval defence (£470 million), and fisheries and aquaculture (£400 million).

⇨ Wind and tidal energy are likely to meet 50% of the UK's renewable energy needs.

The current situation and background

The Government's marine programme covers six areas:

Implementing the Marine Strategy Framework Directive

Defra is implementing the Marine Strategy Framework Directive to secure good environmental status in our seas. This Directive requires EU member states to put in place measures to achieve or maintain good environmental status in their seas by 2020. The Government is transposing the Directive's requirements into national legislation and deciding what good environmental status will mean for our seas, balancing our environmental ambitions against impacts on industry and society as a whole.

Managing our marine resources to secure sustainable development in our seas

The Marine and Coastal Access Act 2009 provides for a planning system and a streamlined licensing system. This will secure sustainable economic growth, balanced with environmental protection and support for communities. With the devolved administrations, Defra is preparing the Marine Policy Statement, which sets the framework for marine plans and provides a coherent approach to the demands and pressures on our seas. New marine plans will be rolled out from 2011 to provide more strategic national and local decision-making to assist sustained economic growth and environmental protection. The Marine Management Organisation, established under the Act in April 2010, brings together management of a number of marine activities including fishing, nature conservation, licensing and enforcement within a single organisation and will also be responsible for the marine planning system.

Protecting, conserving and enhancing marine biodiversity

Defra is seeking to halt the decline in biodiversity, and allow recovery where appropriate. This requires a wide

range of measures to be agreed to meet our obligations under EU and national legislation, while managing competition between conservation and socio-economic needs. Marine protected areas are one of the major tools to conserve biodiversity and associated ecosystem services in the marine environment. We are giving high priority to maintaining the International Whaling Commission's moratorium on commercial whaling.

Securing economically and environmentally sustainable fisheries

We are seeking new ways of managing fisheries at national, European and international levels to secure long-term sustainable fisheries, support a viable fishing industry and provide secure, healthy food supplies. Our work includes seeking radical reform of the Common Fisheries Policy in 2012, reforming English inshore fisheries to deliver a thriving and sustainable inshore fleet, and reducing discards. We are also setting up Inshore Fisheries and Conservation Authorities, under the Marine and Coastal Access Act, to replace Sea Fisheries Committees to modernise inshore fisheries management in England.

Managing fish and seafood supply chain to provide secure, healthy food

We are seeking sustainable consumption and production throughout the fish supply chain. We are contributing to the Defra Food Strategy and Action Plan and taking forward the evidence from the industry-led Fish and Shellfish Roadmap to feed into fisheries reform. We are assessing the potential for increasing domestic shellfish and aquaculture production and we are also supporting a sustainable global fisheries trade, including controls on illegal, unreported and unregulated fishing.

Understanding and adapting to the changing marine environment

As we face serious challenges, such as climate change, ocean acidification and depletion of some fish stocks, high-quality targeted marine science is essential to provide the evidence base for effective policy-making. We are working with European partners to meet the requirements of the EU Marine Strategy Framework Directive and to assess the impacts of climate change on our seas and ways we can adapt to this. The Marine Science Co-ordination Committee is steering UK marine science programmes, including work on climate change. The UK Marine Monitoring and Assessment Strategy community assesses the state of UK seas.

⇨ The above information is reprinted with kind permission from Defra. Visit www.defra.gov.uk for more information.

Floods and droughts

Floods are the most common natural disaster and cause more deaths and damage than any other type. Yet floods also sustain aquatic life and riverine biodiversity, recharge aquifers, enrich soils and, in some of the world's poorest areas, provide an important means of irrigation.

Affects the already vulnerable

One of the most severe by-products of global warming and climate change is increasingly widespread drought, which will affect a large number of nations in the future, especially those in regions already prone to experiencing such phenomena. Droughts have a major impact on food security, especially for vulnerable populations, and also can have major long-term socio-economic impacts. Countries reliant on hydropower for electricity generation experience power shortages. Countries reliant upon rain-fed agriculture can find that the GDP for the country as a whole is significantly reduced in times of drought.

One of the most severe by-products of global warming and climate change is increasingly widespread drought, which will affect a large number of nations in the future

Building resilience

The challenge is to reduce the negative impact of floods and droughts on human lives and livelihoods by reducing the risk of such disasters, and by building resilience of people and communities. Prediction and monitoring are key to developing early warning systems and disaster preparedness. Approaches should be holistic, taking into account the needs of communities, the built environment, and aquatic ecosystems within the catchment or river basin where they occur. Hence water-related disaster management needs to be integrated with other planning spheres at the catchment level, and also address the fact that many poor people live in high-risk locations.

⇨ The above information is reprinted with kind permission from the Global Water Partnership. Visit www.gwp.org for more information.

DEFRA / GLOBAL WATER PARTNERSHIP

'Shocking' new report confirms threats to world's oceans and reefs

Information from the World Resources Institute.

A new report on the state of the world's oceans is gaining considerable attention this week. The report by the International Programme on the State of the Ocean (IPSO) and the International Union for the Conservation of Nature warns that combined threats to oceans are creating conditions where there is 'a high risk of entering a phase of extinction of marine species unprecedented in human history'. Dr Alex Rogers, scientific director of the IPSO, calls the new findings 'shocking'.

While to some this language may seem extreme, the reality is that an unprecedented range of threats are coming together to challenge the health of oceans and underwater life. The report identifies the main drivers of these threats, including: climate change, overexploitation, pollution and habitat loss. The report also finds increasing hypoxia (low oxygen levels) and anoxia (absence of oxygen, known as ocean dead zones) along with warming oceans and increasing acidification are creating multiple stressors on the world's oceans – and multiple stressors are, in their words, a precondition for other mass extinction events in the Earth's history.

The bottom line is that these combined threats – much of it caused by human activity – are undermining the sustainability of our fragile ocean ecosystems, sea life and the value they hold. The World Resources Institute has been working on these issues over its 30-year history – particularly focused on the threats to coral reefs and issues around eutrophication and hypoxia (commonly referred to as 'dead zones').

Coral reefs

Coral reefs are an essential part of ocean ecosystems – home to over 25 per cent of all known species of marine life. The new IPSO report finds that in the past 50 years, activities related to 'overfishing, pollution and unsustainable practices' have led to severe declines in many marine species and an unprecedented level of degradation and loss of critically important habitat types such as mangroves, seagrass meadows and coral reefs. These pressures are being compounded by global warming, which leads to coral bleaching and related threats from ocean acidification.

These findings echo themes from WRI's recent report, *Reefs at Risk Revisited*, which finds that 75 per cent of the world's reefs are already at risk. WRI found that the main local pressures, including overfishing, destructive fishing and pollution, are leading threats to coral reefs. Like the IPSO, WRI looked at global pressures as well, namely global warming, coral bleaching and ocean acidification. WRI found that unless these combined threats are turned back, more than 90 per cent of coral reefs will be at risk by 2030 and all the world's reefs will be threatened by 2050. In addition, WRI found that in the past ten years, threats to coral reefs increased by 30 per cent – showing that the threats to reefs are increasing both in speed and intensity.

Dead zones

The new IPSO report identifies hypoxia as one of the factors which is threatening ocean life. Last year, WRI worked with the Virginia Institute of Marine Science (VIMS) to identify and map areas around the world that are showing signs of eutrophication and hypoxia. The new research identified 535 low-oxygen 'dead zones', only 56 of which can be classified as improving; an additional 248 sites worldwide were identified as

Level of thought given to loss of biodiversity in the UK, 2007, 2009 and 2011

percentage

Legend: 2007, 2009, 2011

Categories: A great deal, A fair amount, A little, None at all, Don't know

Source: Attitudes and knowledge relating to biodiversity and the natural environment, 2007-2011, DEFRA, © Crown copyright

WORLD RESOURCES INSTITUTE

areas of concern that currently exhibit signs of marine eutrophication and are at risk of developing hypoxia. According to our analysis, the number of eutrophic or hypoxic areas have increased from 42 known hypoxic or eutrophic sites in 1950 to the 783 sites we've identified today. This represents an 1,800% increase in eutrophic and hypoxic areas over the past 60 years.

Dead zones are the result of over-fertilisation of our coastal areas from sources such as runoff from agriculture, discharges from industry and human sewage. When a dead zone forms, oxygen in the water is severely depleted – threatening animals, plants and other sea life with it. A combination of stressors from climate change, fisheries, pollution and habitat destruction are leading to more dead zones, further compromising our oceans – including the fragile world of coral reefs.

Cause for hope?

While these findings are grim, there are reasons for hope. The IPSO identifies some key steps that could help reverse the dire direction for our oceans to help restore and protect ocean ecoystems. Their recommendations include:

⇨ reducing carbon emissions;

⇨ restoring the structure and function of marine ecosystems;

⇨ proper and universal implementation of the precautionary principle; and

⇨ urgent introduction by the UN Security Council and the UN General Assembly of effective governance of the high seas.

WRI's research has made it clear that with growing awareness of the declining status of the world's oceans and identifying the most urgent threats and primary drivers of ecosystem degradation, people can take steps to reduce our impact – especially at the local level. Engaging in sustainable business practices (including ecotourism), reducing local pollution (including the over-use of fertilisers), protecting coastal mangroves, establishing more fish sanctuaries and strengthening marine protected areas, as well as improved fisheries management, can all help to buy time for coral reefs.

Supporting comprehensive national assessments to identify the root causes of species decline and degradation of ecosystem services, and mobilise support for urgently-needed policy and institutional reforms, improvements in regulatory frameworks and market-led economic incentives, can help to turn the tide.

On a global level, however, the threats from climate change loom large – more political will is needed, along with more action by governments to prevent the worst possible forecasts of the *State of the Oceans Report*. It is up to people, policymakers and international leaders to make decisions today to ensure that the truly frightening predictions of mass extinction of sea life do not come to pass.

22 June 2011

⇨ The above information is reprinted with kind permission from the World Resources Institute. Visit http://insights.wri.org for more information on this and other related topics.

© *World Resources Institute*

Population and the environment: where we're headed and what we can do

Many environmental problems will be easier to address if world population peaks at eight billion rather than continuing to grow to 11 billion or higher. The good news: there is already a global consensus on how to slow population growth, with programmes that improve human wellbeing at very little cost.

POPULATION ACTION INTERNATIONAL

World population is still growing

While the rate of population growth has slowed in most parts of the world, overall growth continues. We increase by nearly 80 million people every year – the numerical equivalent of adding another US to the world every four years. The number of people on the planet has doubled since 1960 and will reach seven billion in 2011.

Tomorrow's population size will be determined today

We often hear the prediction that world population will reach nine billion in 2050, but demographers project a range of possibilities – from eight billion to 11 billion by mid-century. By 2100, the range is even wider – from six billion to 16 billion. Tomorrow's population size depends on the choices couples make about childbearing today, but far too many lack the means to plan and space their pregnancies. Around the world, 215 million women want to prevent pregnancy but need contraception. In nations where access to contraception is limited – such as Yemen, Afghanistan and much of Sub-Saharan Africa – women continue to have an average of more than five children. And the need for contraception is growing. Nearly half the world's population is under the age of 25 and entering their childbearing years.

Eight billion would be better than 11 billion – for people and the planet

The impact of population growth on the environment is mediated by consumption, technology, urbanisation and other factors. Still, slower population growth could reduce pressure on natural systems that are already over-taxed, and research shows that a host of environmental problems – including the growth of greenhouse gases, water scarcity and biodiversity loss – would be easier to

address if world population peaks at eight billion, rather than climbing to 11 billion or more. Climate change is expected to result in declining agricultural production in many parts of the world, and will make limited water supplies even more difficult to manage. Slower population growth would help people adapt to climate change, reduce the scale of human vulnerability to these impacts, and give nations a chance to make essential investments in healthcare, education and sustainable economic development.

The good news: we know how to slow population growth

A half-century of experience has shown that the best way to slow growth is to ensure that people are able to make decisions about childbearing. That means providing access to contraception and other reproductive health services, not 'population control' measures that could become coercive. It means education and employment opportunities, especially for women. And it means tackling gender and economic inequities that are associated with rapid population growth.

There are success stories: international family planning programmes, supported by the US, have enabled women around the world to plan and space their pregnancies. Partly as a result of those programmes, contraceptive use in developing countries rose from less than ten per cent in the 1960s to 60 per cent today, and fertility rates fell from six children per woman to three. But with 215 million women around the world still in need of contraceptives, the job is not yet done.

There is already a global agreement on population and development goals

The world's nations are struggling for consensus on climate change but we already have a UN agreement on

population, endorsed by 179 developed and developing nations in 1994 in Cairo. Countries at that time agreed on a plan to slow population growth through universal access to reproductive health services, empowering girls and women, and combating poverty. These were reaffirmed in the UN Millennium Development Goals earlier this decade.

A half-century of experience has shown that the best way to slow growth is to ensure that people are able to make decisions about childbearing

---

Domestically, despite some politicians' attempts to politicise the issue, the American public is overwhelmingly supportive of family planning. In multiple polls over decades, 75 to 90 per cent of Americans support international family planning programmes, including 69 per cent of Independents and Republicans.

Family planning programmes are cost-effective and contribute to human wellbeing

Family planning programmes are relatively inexpensive, especially when compared to many environmental mitigation efforts. Meeting the demand for family planning in the developing world would require an additional $3.6 billion annually. The US share of the cost is about $1 billion. These programmes also support broader US foreign policy and development goals and make enormous contributions to human health and wellbeing. Meeting the need for family planning would help millions adapt to climate change, and prevent 53 million unintended pregnancies, 150,000 maternal deaths and 25 million abortions.

But governments are not keeping their promises

Despite the low cost and many benefits of family planning programmes, the world's nations have yet to mobilise sufficient resources to pay for them. While developing countries are spending about half of what they pledged in Cairo, developed countries have provided less than a quarter of the promised funding. US support for international family planning assistance has increased from $464 million in 2008 to $615 million in 2011, but further increases are needed to address rising need. The 2010 US funding level is nearly 25 per cent less (adjusted for inflation) than the 1995 level, despite the fact that the number of women of reproductive age in the developing world has grown by more than 300 million since then.

Environmentalists have an important role to play

Since the 1970s, environmentalists have been an important constituency for US leadership in population policy. A family planning vote has been a part of the League of Conservation Voters scorecard since 1985. But greater effort is needed to incorporate population and family planning into global and national environmental dialogues. Drawing these connections can keep the pressure on Washington to increase funding for international family planning assistance. A broad coalition of environmentalists, reproductive health and rights organisations, faith groups and relief and development organisations are calling on Congress and the Administration to increase funding for international family planning to $1 billion. More voices are needed to demonstrate the broad base of support for these vital programmes that benefit human health and wellbeing, as well as the global environment.

Simple points about population and the environment

⇨ Rapid population growth increases pressure on resources that are already over-taxed, including water, forests, land and the atmosphere. If current population growth rates continue, the world's population would grow from around seven billion today to 11 billion by 2050.

⇨ The rate of population growth in the future responds to actions we take today, including providing access to family planning.

⇨ More than 215 million women around the world want to avoid pregnancy but need contraception.

⇨ Achieving universal access to family planning and reproductive health services will improve the health and wellbeing of women and families. Slowing population growth will also ease pressure on natural resources and improve prospects for solving environmental challenges.

⇨ Family planning stands out as an opportunity to improve the health of women and children, while increasing people's resilience to environmental challenges.

⇨ The above information is reprinted with kind permission from Population Action International. Visit www.populationaction.org for more information on this and other related topics.

© *Population Action International*

Demographic change and the environment

An extract from a report by the Royal Commission on Environmental Pollution.

In 2009, the Royal Commission on Environmental Pollution announced that it would investigate the environmental implications of demographic change, looking at the next 40 years to 2050. The Commission chose to study this topic because although there may be a growing understanding of the ways in which the UK population is changing – and much thought is already being given to the social and economic implications of these changes – it seemed that little attention had so far been paid to their environmental consequences. The Commission decided that this was an area in which it could make a useful and timely contribution.

The basic demographic facts are that, since the Population Panel reported in 1973, the population of the UK has grown steadily – from 55.9 million in 1971 to 61.8 million in 2009. This trend is likely to continue: the Office for National Statistics (ONS) has published projections suggesting that the population could be 71.6 million in 2033. Within the overall figure, there are a number of important trends – in particular, a significant increase in the number of people over 85 years old, and an even bigger increase in the number of households, particularly one-person households.

> **The basic demographic facts are that, since the Population Panel reported in 1973, the population of the UK has grown steadily – from 55.9 million in 1971 to 61.8 million in 2009**

Perhaps even more crucially, demographic pressures vary in different parts of the UK. Some areas are expected to grow significantly faster than others, whereas in some parts of the UK the population has been decreasing and may continue to decline. In the course of our study, the Commission made several visits and received a large amount of evidence which illustrated just how significant these variations are. There are differences in fertility rates, average lifespan and inward and outward migration between the countries of the UK and their regions, so the demographic profiles of each country and region are different and will evolve in a variety of ways.

The Commission also found significant variations at a more local scale.

Overview

Current trends suggest we can expect a growing population in the UK – fuelled by increasing life expectancy and net inward migration – and an increasing number of households, more of them occupied by only one person. But these trends do not apply uniformly across the UK and we were struck by the intense graininess of the situation at all levels. Where people are, and how they live, have major environmental impacts. More importantly, policies to influence behaviour and consumption may be more effective than any attempt to constrain or even reduce population size.

Demographic pressures vary in different parts of the UK

We found that the sheer number of people is not likely to be the most significant influence on environmental quality in the UK over the next 40 years: the impact of any population on the environment is mediated by the way people live – their consumption patterns, the energy and water they use, and the waste they generate. If we are serious about reducing the impact of population on the environment, these issues need to be given at least as much attention as overall numbers. There is a relationship between the size of the population and certain basic environmental services, such as water supply and quality, energy use and waste generation. But we found that this relationship was not as clear as might be expected. We were also surprised that, to the extent that they were aware of the challenges ahead, public bodies and service providers had to cope with very varied circumstances and were preparing for them in a range of different ways. As mentioned, the way population is distributed is crucial to any understanding of environmental impact – where people live, work and travel affects the environment in the broadest sense and this suggests that there needs to be a thorough evaluation of the role of the planning system to ensure that proper account is taken of the impact of growth or depopulation.

February 2011

⇨ The above information is an extract from the Royal Commission on Environmental Pollution's report *Demographic change and the environment*, and is reprinted with permission. Visit www.rcep.org.uk for more.

ROYAL COMMISSION ON ENVIRONMENTAL POLLUTION

Urgent action needed to redesign the food system due to the world's growing population

A new report, published today by Foresight, the Government's futures think tank, argues for fundamental change to the global food system if a rapidly expanding global population is to be fed over the next 40 years.

The Foresight project 'Global Food and Farming Futures' has examined how a rapidly expanding global population can be fed in a healthy and sustainable way. Multiple threats are converging on the food system, including changes in the climate, competition for resources such as water supply and energy, and changing consumption patterns provide considerable challenges to sustaining the world's food supply.

Professor Sir John Beddington, the Government's Chief Scientific Adviser and head of the Foresight programme, said:

'The Foresight study shows that the food system is already failing in at least two ways. Firstly, it is unsustainable, with resources being used faster than they can be naturally replenished. Secondly, a billion people are going hungry with another billion people suffering from "hidden hunger", whilst a billion people are over-consuming.

'The project has helped to identify a wide range of possible actions that can meet the challenges facing food and farming, both now and in the future.'

The report's main findings are:

⇨ Threat of hunger could increase: efforts to end hunger internationally are already stalling, and without decisive action food prices could rise substantially over the next 40 years, making the situation worse. This will affect us all – as more of the world suffers from hunger, social tensions will increase, as will the threat of conflict and migration. Wider economic growth will also be affected.

⇨ The global food system is living outside its means, consuming resources faster than they are naturally replenished. It must be redesigned to bring sustainability centre stage: substantial changes will be required throughout the food system and related areas, such as water use, energy use and addressing climate change, if food security is to be provided for a predicted nine billion or more people out to 2050.

⇨ There is no quick fix: the potential threats converging on the global food system are so great that action is needed across many fronts, from changing diets to eliminating food waste.

Professor Beddington added:

'With the global population set to rise and food prices likely to increase, it is crucial that a wide range of complementary actions from policy makers, farmers and businesses are taken now. Urgent change is required throughout the food system to bring sustainability centre stage and end hunger. It is also vital for other areas, such as climate change mitigation, conflict and economic growth.'

Three important areas for change include:

⇨ Minimising waste in all areas of the food system: an amount of food equivalent to about a quarter of today's annual production could potentially be saved by 2050 if the current estimate of global food waste is halved.

⇨ Balancing future demand and supply in the food system: this could include helping businesses to measure the environmental impacts of food so that consumers can choose products that promote sustainability.

FORESIGHT

⇨ Improving governance of the global food system: it is important to reduce subsidies and trade barriers that disadvantage poor countries. The project's economic modelling shows how trade restrictions can amplify shocks in the food system, raising prices further.

The challenges identified in the report show an urgent need to link food and agriculture policy to wider global governance agendas such as climate change mitigation, biodiversity and international development. Without this link a decision in one area could compromise important objectives in another.

'The food price crisis in 2008 increased the number of people suffering from hunger by 150 million'

The report, sponsored by the Department for Environment, Food and Rural Affairs and the Department for International Development, outlines the findings of an extensive two-year study. It has involved around 400 experts from about 35 countries and considered food and farming in oceans and freshwater environments as well as on the land.

Environment Secretary Caroline Spelman said:

'We need a global, integrated approach to food security, one that looks beyond the food system to the inseparable goals of reducing poverty, tackling climate change and reducing biodiversity loss – and the UK Government is determined to show the international leadership needed to make that happen.

'We can unlock an agricultural revolution in the developing world, which would benefit the poorest the most, simply by improving access to knowledge and technology, creating better access to markets and investing in infrastructure.

'To fuel this revolution, we must open up global markets, boost global trade and make reforms that help the poorest. Trade restrictions must be avoided, especially at times of scarcity. And we must manage price volatility by building trust and cooperation – and in particular by creating greater transparency around the true levels of food stocks.'

International Development Secretary Andrew Mitchell said:

'With one-seventh of the world's population still hungry, this report is a clarion call to arms. The food price crisis in 2008 increased the number of people suffering from hunger by 150 million. Today, reports of increasing food prices once again fill the news – and it's clear from this new study that price volatility is only set to increase in the future, making further food price spikes inevitable.

'Internationally, those with the least spend the largest proportion of their income on food, so food price shocks hit the poorest hardest and can have long-term impacts on their health. Britain is already working to tackle malnutrition, improve agriculture, and get new research into the hands of the poorest people. Steps taken now and pushed through over the next few decades to stabilise global markets, reduce volatility and prioritise agriculture will have a disproportionate effect on ensuring food security for a predicted nine billion people by 2050.'

24 January 2011

⇨ The above information is reprinted with kind permission from Foresight. Visit www.bis.gov.uk/foresight for more information.

© Crown copyright

FORESIGHT

Water and sanitation

The achievement of providing 1.8 billion people with access to safe drinking water since 1990 is diminished by the absence of matching investment in sanitation. The lack of hygienic facilities experienced by 2.6 billion people is a fundamental cause of disease which leads to 1.4 million child deaths each year. Climate change uncertainties cast a menacing shadow over the efforts of developing countries to honour their citizens' rights to safe water and sanitation.

Millennium Development Goals

Global water and sanitation data is published by the UN every two years. The 2010 update presents the drinking water target as one of the few success stories of the Millennium Development Goals (MDGs) programme. Aggregate global coverage has advanced from 77% to 87% between 1990 and 2008, very close to the 2015 target of 88%.

However, the inclusion of rich countries in these statistics conceals the less rosy picture in much of the developing world. According to a 2010 UNEP report, only 26 out of 53 countries in Africa are likely to reach the MDG target for drinking water.

Global access to safe sanitation increased only from 54% to 61% in the period 1990-2008, leaving 2.6 billion people unprotected

The wording of the MDG calls on governments to 'halve, by 2015, the proportion of people without sustainable access to safe drinking water and sanitation'.

A source which separates the delivery of drinking water from potential contamination, such as a piped supply or a protected well or spring, is deemed to be 'safe'. Interpretation of 'access' has varied between countries but generally refers to a household supply of 20 litres that can be fetched within a 30-minute round trip, a distance of about one kilometre.

Simple low-cost, low-maintenance technologies are available to fulfil these undemanding criteria. Yet almost 900 million people are forced to gamble their health with unsafe drinking water.

Published on behalf of the UN by the WHO/UNICEF Joint Monitoring Programme for Water Supply and Sanitation, the 2010 update is also the first to confirm longstanding fears that the explosion of urban populations in poorer countries is too fast for municipal authorities to keep up. Global access to safe water in urban areas fell back slightly from 95% to 94% between 2006 and 2008.

Some water sector specialists are concerned about the absence of qualitative indicators to support these measures of coverage. Some regions are prone to chemical pollution (as in China) or natural contamination (as in the arsenic crisis in parts of South Asia).

Neglect of sanitation and hygiene

Defined as a facility which removes excreta from the risk of human contact, 'safe' sanitation encompasses covered pit latrines as well as flush toilets.

Since its belated addition to the MDGs in 2002, the sanitation target has been the Cinderella of the cause, attracting little over 10% of funds available for water and sanitation programmes. More Africans have access to mobile phones than toilets. The same is true in India, a country which boasts nuclear weapons and a space programme.

Development agencies must accept some responsibility, their publicity cameras preferring to linger on happy children pumping water. Latrines offer less inspiring images and copy. Even the UN's declaration of the period 2005-2015 as the 'International Decade for Action – Water for Life' betrayed neglect of sanitation, in presentation if not intent.

The consequence is that global access to safe sanitation increased only from 54% to 61% in the period 1990-2008, leaving 2.6 billion people unprotected. This figure has barely changed in recent years, dooming the 2015 MDG target to almost certain failure.

In Sub-Saharan Africa, progress from 26% to 31% extrapolates to arrive at the target sometime during the 22nd century. Although the incidence of open defecation in South Asia has reduced by a third since 1990, 700 million people in the region continue to suffer this indignity.

The UN corrected its earlier omission by proclaiming 2008 as the Year of Sanitation and the development agencies have overhauled their presentations.

For example, the familiar statement that diarrhoea is caused by drinking contaminated water presents an incomplete picture. More attention is now given to the

ONEWORLD UK

link with unsafe sanitation and absence of hand-washing. Diarrhoea is a significant cause of child mortality.

Strategic and operational problems

The UN 2010 Global Annual Assessment of Sanitation and Drinking Water reports that the proportion of total foreign aid allocated to the sector fell from 8% to 5% between 1997 and 2008. Furthermore, less than half of this aid is directed to the Least Developed Countries where the need is greatest.

Developing countries, too, are guilty of attaching insufficient priority to water, and even less to sanitation, in national poverty reduction plans. Budgets are typically less than 0.5% of GDP and coordination between ministries poor. The limited capacity of national and local government departments to implement projects at village level has not been assisted by the abundance of uncoordinated donor programmes.

There is a deeper problem than shortage of finance. *The Global Corruption Report 2008,* published by Transparency International, warned that 'corruption in the water sector is a root cause and catalyst for the global water crisis'.

It traces how funds are diverted at every level of project implementation so that the proportion of aid actually invested is alarmingly low. In urban projects, petty corruption is notorious for forcing up water charges.

The right to water and sanitation

The Universal Declaration of Human Rights and its relevant legal embodiment, the International Covenant on Economic, Social and Cultural Rights, refer to the right to an adequate 'standard of living', without elaboration.

Years of campaigning to capture the right to water and sanitation within this broad terminology eventually came to fruition in a resolution passed by the UN General Assembly in July 2010. It recognised 'the right to safe and clean drinking water and sanitation as a human right that is essential for the full enjoyment of life and all human rights'.

International and national laws dealing with human rights should now recognise the right to water and sanitation as equal to other basic rights such as food. Nevertheless, whilst unquestionably a milestone in global justice and a boost to the moral authority of campaigners, the UN resolution remains distant from political processes responsible for protecting the poor through legislation.

Progressive countries such as South Africa and Uruguay have anticipated the ruling by acknowledging the right to water in their constitutions, but these remain a minority.

Wider recognition of water as a right rather than a commodity might have prevented the privatisation of many municipal water supplies in developing countries over the last two decades. Commercial suppliers consistently favour middle-class households at the expense of poorer peri-urban settlements. This mismatch led to many failures of private capital and confrontation with authorities.

A rights perspective also illustrates the weakness of the MDG programme. Its focus on halving numbers who lack water and sanitation, as opposed to achieving universal access, denies the rights of 1.7 billion people who will remain without sanitation, and 800 million without drinking water, even if the MDG targets are met in 2015.

Solutions

Principled debate about rights is valuable but it is the economics of water and sanitation that has the potential to make an immediate difference. The cost of inaction is impossible to defend.

Economic opportunities are lost in the time spent fetching water, in girls staying away from school due to the lack of toilet facilities, and in treating illnesses caused by poor sanitation and hygiene. Progress in water and sanitation contributes directly to broader MDG targets for child mortality, gender equity, universal education and poverty reduction.

This multiplier effect is confirmed in studies which show that each $1 of investment in providing safe water yields over $4, whilst the corresponding investment in sanitation delivers a staggering $9 return.

Such results reinforce the 2006 UN Human Development Report which estimated that failure to invest in water and sanitation was costing Sub-Saharan Africa about 5% of GDP. A 2010 World Bank study puts a huge price of $54 billion, 6.4% of GDP, on India's poor state of sanitation, including the loss of tourism revenues.

Potential financial returns of this order would provoke frenzy within private capital markets. But the international donor community provides barely half of UNICEF's relatively modest estimate of $11.3 billion per annum to achieve the water and sanitation MDG targets for all developing countries.

One attempt to overcome this lethargy is 'Sanitation and Water for All'. This initiative facilitates high-level meetings between donor and recipient governments 'to gain a greater understanding of the linkages between water, sanitation, and economic growth, in order to commit the appropriate resources'.

Action at village level is just as important. There has to be greater determination in convincing households of the value of safe sanitation and improved hygiene.

Offering government subsidies for latrine construction has been notoriously unsuccessful.

Promising results have been achieved in an approach known as community-led sanitation, which promotes behaviour change through peer group condemnation of open defecation as an anti-social habit.

Creating a sense of ownership within community-level water and sanitation projects in both rural and urban areas has a consistent record of success. Whilst it is difficult to convert small-scale developments into national programmes, an improved understanding of the right to water could translate into wider citizenship movements to bring local and national governments to account.

Water scarcity

Under pressure from rising populations, more extravagant lifestyles, intensive agriculture and industrialisation, water has become a scarce resource. Inevitably, it is the poor who tend to lose out in competition for resources, typically through the pricing mechanism.

The World Bank estimates that demand for water will exceed supply by 40% by 2030. UN Water suggests that 1.8 billion people live in regions already classified as water scarce. Two thirds of the global population could experience water stress by 2025.

Those who applaud the world's achievement of expanding food production exponentially over the last generation tend to forget the parallel demands placed on water resources. Many countries extract freshwater faster than its natural rate of replenishment, causing groundwater tables to fall dramatically.

The productivity of a quarter of the world's rice-growing regions may be at risk by 2025. A new industry in efficient irrigation devices is booming as the combined imperatives of food and water security become ever more apparent.

Even if the international donor community delivers all the funding requested for safe drinking water, the MDG targets could still fail through inadequate integration with the bigger water picture. Domestic water use amounts to only 8% of overall global consumption, tiny in comparison with agriculture at 70% and industry at 22%.

'Integrated water resources management' describes the demanding ideal of accommodating these three user categories within the overarching goal of environmental sustainability. Even if local tensions can be resolved, the water cycle itself is blind to national boundaries, creating immense difficulties for bilateral and multilateral reconciliation of competing demands.

The significance of the manufacturing industry is not just its rising water consumption but also that the goods produced may not be enjoyed by the country which provided the water. Globalisation is moving this virtual water around the world, often from countries which can ill afford its loss. For example, production of one cotton shirt requires 2,700 litres of water.

The omission of the cost of virtual water bears witness to another failure of modern market economics. Attempts are underway to quantify this water footprint for labelling purposes.

Many of the world's largest cities are replicating the unsustainable culture of rural economies by over-extraction of vital aquifers. However, nowhere is the need for demand management more acute than the Middle East. Annual per capita use in countries such as Yemen and Syria has fallen as low as 200-300 cubic metres, far below the international scarcity guideline of 1,700 cubic metres.

Measures found across the region include awareness programmes, water pricing, pollution prevention, and recycled wastewater. The ultimate irony of water management in the 21st century is the increasing interest in restoration of traditional storage technologies, many of them dating from antiquity.

Climate change

The stresses already imposed on water security and access to drinking water will be accentuated by climate change. Almost a third of the World Bank's long-term water projects are assessed to be at risk from changes in water run-off by 2030.

Every headline impact of global warming has resonance for the planet's hydrological cycle. The volume and timing of water flows within individual ecosystems will be affected by disturbance to rainfall patterns and accelerated thawing of glaciers. Water quality in coastal regions will be prone to saline intrusion as sea levels rise.

Some regions will become wetter and others drier; unfortunately the 'losers' in this transition will be the poorer countries. It is no surprise that the significant majority of priority projects identified by these countries in their National Adaptation Programmes of Action (NAPAs) address issues related to water.

Updated April 2011

⇨ This is an extract from the *OneWorld (water and sanitation) guide*, published by OneWorld UK in its range of educational guides on global issues at http://uk.oneworld.net/guides

ONEWORLD UK

Reducing water wastage in the UK

Information from Waterwise.

Why is water an issue?

You may wonder why saving water is important, as it appears to rain all the time in the UK. Wet summers and even wetter winters seem to keep the garden nice and green and our rivers flowing. Despite having a seemingly wet climate, some parts of the UK are experiencing water shortages. The south-east of England has less water available per person than the Sudan and Syria.

It is not feasible for us to give our water to parts of the world where they are suffering serious droughts, so surely it should be OK for us to use all our water? Yes: Waterwise doesn't want people to stop using water, we want people to stop wasting water. The key to water efficiency is reducing waste, not restricting use. About one-third of the water each person uses on a daily basis is wasted – it runs straight down the plughole or down the toilet without being used. It is this wastage we want to cut down.

Why save water? The facts

The UK has less available water per person than most other European countries. London is drier than Istanbul, and the south-east of England has less water available per person than the Sudan and Syria.

Water is scarce in parts of Scotland, Wales and Northern Ireland as well as in England – large-scale drought is already occurring in the UK, with the lowest rainfall, groundwater and reservoir levels for decades.

Each person in the UK uses 150 litres of water a day. This takes into account cooking, cleaning, washing and flushing. This has been rising by 1% a year since 1930. This consumption level is not sustainable in the long term.

If we do not take action now, climate change, population shifts and behaviour mean the UK will face increased water stress in the future.

Waterwise is currently carrying out cost-benefit analysis on the advantages of demand-side measures rather than supply-side measures. It is Waterwise's opinion that water efficiency and water meters, when combined with improving leaks from water mains, are more cost-effective and better for the environment than building new reservoirs to increase the supply of water.

The water cycle is continuous and it will rain and replace water that has been abstracted for use in the home; however, there is no guarantee where and when the rain will fall, and your supply might be depleted before the next downpour.

Saving water will not only save the environment, but if you are on a water meter it will save you money on your water bill, and it will save you money on your energy bill if you reduce your hot water consumption.

Waterwise has carried out some research and found that the energy used to pump, treat and heat the water in the average family's home produces the carbon equivalent of a return flight from London to New York. These carbon emissions are a global problem, because they are aggravating the effects of climate change. Therefore, saving water will also help alleviate climate change and can make the water scarcity problem in another country less severe. So, even though we cannot help other nations by transporting our water to them, we can help them by reducing our carbon emissions by wasting less hot water.

Why save water? The figures

A running tap uses six litres of water a minute, a shower can use anywhere between nine and 45 litres per minute, a hosepipe uses as much as 1,000 litres per hour.

Toilet flushing accounts for 30% of our daily water use – with old toilets using as much as 14 litres per flush compared to new dual flush models, which use as little as 2.6 and four litres per flush.

Fixing a dripping tap can save as much as 5,000 litres a year – if everyone in the UK fixed their dripping taps we would save enough water to supply 120,000 for one day.

How to save water: the tips

There are numerous ways you can save water. You can purchase water-efficient products and install them. This means you can fix and forget. You can install the product, and you don't have to alter your behaviour in any way. However, there are also things that you can do for free which save water.

Turn the tap off when you brush your teeth

A running tap wastes six litres of water a minute. If everyone in the UK who currently leaves the tap running when they brush their teeth turned it off instead, we would save 446 million litres of water – enough water to supply 2.9 million people for one day. That's the entire population of Leeds, Birmingham, Glasgow and Sheffield (the UK's 2nd, 3rd, 4th and 5th largest cities) for one whole day.

Don't use your toilet as a dustbin

An unnecessary flush uses another cistern full of water. Put your face wipes and cotton wool balls in your dustbin rather than down the toilet. If everyone in the UK who currently uses their toilet as a dustbin stopped doing this, we would save 27 million litres of water a week – that's enough to supply the population of York or Portsmouth for one day.

Use the leftover water from your night-time drinks to water houseplants

This saves new water being poured into the plants and your drink being poured down the plughole.

Invest in a water butt and connect it to your drainpipe in your garden

This can then collect some of the 85,000 litres of rainfall that falls on your roof every year. This water can be used to water your garden, clean your car and wash your windows.

Install a cistern displacement device in your toilet

These can be obtained free of charge from your water company and displace water in your cistern so that the volume of water in your flush is reduced by between one and three litres. Please note that you do not need a cistern displacement device if you have a dual flush toilet.

The average Briton really consumes over 3,400 litres every day

---

Embedded water

The average Briton really consumes over 3,400 litres every day! This amount includes the water we use daily in our homes, but it also includes the amount embedded in all that we consume.

Water is hidden in all that we see: in our cars, our clothing, and in our sandwiches. But we can significantly and easily reduce our water footprints. We can buy water-efficient white goods, turn off the tap while we brush our teeth, fix leaks, and make many other easy efforts.

We can start asking shops to provide information on how much water is embedded in their products. And we can ask our leaders to make water-use efficiency across all sectors of society a priority.

⇨ The above information is reprinted with kind permission from Waterwise. Visit www.waterwise.org.uk for more information.

© Waterwise

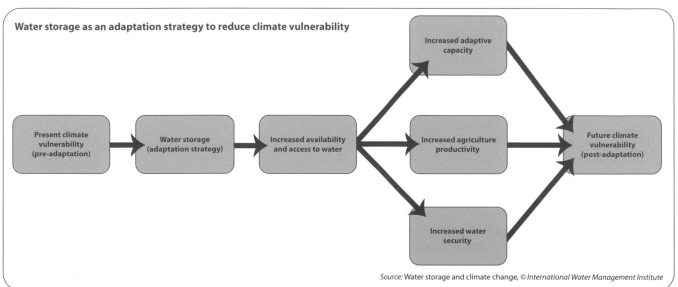

Water storage as an adaptation strategy to reduce climate vulnerability

Present climate vulnerability (pre-adaptation) → Water storage (adaptation strategy) → Increased availability and access to water → Increased adaptive capacity / Increased agriculture productivity / Increased water security → Future climate vulnerability (post-adaptation)

Source: Water storage and climate change, © International Water Management Institute

WATERWISE

Water statistics

Statistical information from WaterAid.

A global crisis

⇨ 884 million people in the world do not have access to safe water. This is roughly one in eight of the world's population. (WHO/UNICEF)

⇨ 2.6 billion people in the world do not have access to adequate sanitation. This is almost two-fifths of the world's population. (WHO/UNICEF)

⇨ 1.4 million children die every year from diarrhoea caused by unclean water and poor sanitation – 4,000 child deaths a day or one child every 20 seconds. This equates to 160 infant school classrooms lost every single day to an entirely preventable public health crisis. (WHO/WaterAid)

What has WaterAid done?

⇨ Since 1981, we have reached 15.89 million people with safe water.

⇨ Since 2004, we have reached 11.02 million people with sanitation.

⇨ In 2010/11 we reached 1.45 million people with safe water and 1.62 million people with sanitation.

⇨ Just £15 can enable one person to access a lasting supply of safe water, improved hygiene and sanitation. (WaterAid)

Sanitation

⇨ Diarrhoea kills more children every year than AIDS, malaria and measles combined. (WHO)

⇨ Children living in households with no toilet are twice as likely to get diarrhoea as those with a toilet. (WEDC)

⇨ Every year, around 60 million children in the developing world are born into households without access to sanitation. (UN Water)

⇨ One gram of human faeces can contain 10,000,000 viruses, 1,000,000 bacteria, 1,000 parasite cysts, 100 parasite eggs. (UNICEF)

⇨ At any given time, close to half the people in the developing world are suffering from one or more of the main diseases associated with dirty water and inadequate sanitation, such as diarrhoea, guinea worm, trachoma and schistosomiasis. (UNDP Human Development Report 2006)

⇨ Half the hospital beds in developing countries are filled with people suffering from diseases associated with poor water, sanitation and hygiene. (UNDP Human Development Report 2006)

Hygiene

⇨ Hand-washing with soap at critical times can reduce the incidence of diarrhoea by up to 47%. (UN Water)

⇨ The integrated approach of providing water, sanitation and hygiene reduces the number of deaths caused by diarrhoeal diseases by an average of 65%. (WHO)

Water

⇨ The weight of water that women in Africa and Asia carry on their heads is commonly 20 kg, the same as the average UK airport luggage allowance. (HDR)

⇨ The average person in the developing world uses ten litres of water every day for their drinking, washing and cooking. (WSSCC)

⇨ The average European uses 200 litres of water every day for their drinking, washing and cooking. North Americans use 400 litres. (HDR)

⇨ On current trends, over the next 20 years humans will use 40% more water than they do now. (UNEP)

⇨ Agriculture accounts for over 80% of the world's water consumption. (UNEP)

⇨ 97.5% of the Earth's water is saltwater. If the world's water fitted into a bucket, only one teaspoonful would be drinkable. (HDR)

Education and livelihoods

⇨ For every $1 invested in water and sanitation, on average $8 is returned in increased productivity. (UNDP)

⇨ Lack of safe water and sanitation costs Sub-Saharan Africa around 5% of its Gross Domestic Product (GDP) each year. (UNDP)

Millennium Development Goals

⇨ The world is on track to meet or even exceed the MDG for safe drinking water – to halve the proportion of people without access to safe water by 2015. However, even though we are on track globally, 884 million people are still without access. (WHO/UNICEF)

⇨ The world is seriously off track to meet the sanitation MDG target – to halve the proportion of people

WATERAID

without access to sanitation by 2015. If current rates of progress continue, the global sanitation goal will be met 30 years too late. In Sub-Saharan Africa, the sanitation target in that region is not due to be met for another 200 years. (WHO/UNICEF)

⇨ Nearly half the people who gained access to water between 1990 and 2008 live in India and China. (WHO/UNICEF)

Financing the sector

⇨ Over the past ten years, aid to health and HIV/AIDS in Sub-Saharan Africa has increased by nearly 500%, while aid to water and sanitation has increased by only 79%. (OECD)

Water and sanitation in history

⇨ South Korea made huge investments in water and sanitation during the 1960s, when its per capita income was the same as Ghana's, and during that decade, under-five mortality more than halved, while the number of medical staff stayed virtually the same. (WaterAid)

⇨ In the UK, the expansion of water and sanitation infrastructure in the 1880s contributed to a 15-year increase in life expectancy in the following four decades. (HDR, 2006)

⇨ Information from WaterAid. Visit www.wateraid.org for more.

© WaterAid

Biodegradable products may be bad for the environment

Research from North Carolina State University shows that so-called biodegradable products are likely doing more harm than good in landfills, because they are releasing a powerful greenhouse gas as they break down.

Biodegradable materials, such as disposable cups and utensils, are broken down in landfills by microorganisms that then produce methane, says Dr Morton Barlaz, co-author of a paper describing the research, and professor and head of NC State's Department of Civil, Construction, and Environmental Engineering. 'Methane can be a valuable energy source when captured, but is a potent greenhouse gas when released into the atmosphere,' he adds.

And the US Environmental Protection Agency (EPA) estimates that only about 35 per cent of municipal solid waste goes to landfills that capture methane for energy use. EPA estimates that another 34 per cent of landfills capture methane and burn it off on-site, while 31 per cent allow the methane to escape.

'Methane can be a valuable energy source when captured, but is a potent greenhouse gas when released into the atmosphere'

'In other words,' Barlaz says, 'biodegradable products are not necessarily more environmentally friendly when disposed in landfills.'

This problem may be exacerbated by the rate at which these human-made biodegradable materials break down. Federal Trade Commission (FTC) guidelines call for products marked as 'biodegradable'

to decompose within 'a reasonably short period of time' after disposal. But such rapid degradation may actually be environmentally harmful, because federal regulations do not require landfills that collect methane to install gas collection systems for at least two years after the waste is buried. If materials break down and release methane quickly, much of that methane will likely be emitted before the collection technology is installed. This means less potential fuel for energy use, and more greenhouse gas emissions.

As a result, the researchers find that a slower rate of biodegradation is actually more environmentally friendly, because the bulk of the methane production will occur after the methane collection system is in place. Some specific biodegradable products, such as bags that hold yard waste and are always sent to composting or anaerobic digestion facilities, were not included in the study.

'If we want to maximise the environmental benefit of biodegradable products in landfills,' Barlaz says, 'we need to both expand methane collection at landfills and design these products to degrade more slowly – in contrast to FTC guidance.'

1 June 2011

⇨ The above information is reprinted with kind permission from Matt Shipman, North Carolina State University. Visit www.ncsu.edu for more.

© North Carolina State University

Rising tide of drugs and medicines polluting EU waters

Information from EurActiv.com

Europe's freshwaters are increasingly filled with pharmaceutical residues and other micro-pollutants, which are potentially harmful to human health and the environment, according to Friedrich Barth from the European Water Partnership (EWP), an industry-backed group.

'One of the big problems in Europe will be micro-pollution – from pharmaceuticals, but also from pesticides and nutrients,' said Barth, whose organisation brings together water treatment industries, governments, researchers and NGOs.

Pollution from invisible emerging chemical pollutants like nanoparticles were highlighted as a growing concern at this year's World Water Week in Stockholm.

The chemicals can range from pesticides to flame retardants, steroids and hormones from birth-control pills.

Residues from pharmaceuticals in particular are set to become a hot topic in the future, Barth predicted, noting that there is currently no EU legislation that addresses the issue.

'This is an area that has to be addressed in a much better way,' he stressed.

Emerging pollutants

Emerging pollutants include hormones from birth-control pills, which researchers say have feminising effects on the male fish population in rivers and lakes all over the world, threatening reproduction and food security.

They also include residues of antibiotics, anti-depressants, tranquilisers and cancer treatments, which find their way into the water cycle via different pathways.

Some of these pollutants might be carcinogenic or have environmental effects. 'The worst is of course if it goes into drinking water,' Barth said.

'One immediate measure would be to address waste water from hospitals. It needs to be collected separately,' he suggested.

But this might not be the perfect solution as people use drugs at home as well, making micro-pollution a pervasive issue.

'Clearly, more research on the matter is needed, the "end-of-pipe" water issue needs to be considered already during the pharmaceutical development phase, and the substances monitored already before the water enters a treatment plant,' Barth suggested.

A spokesperson for EFPIA, a trade group representing the European pharmaceutical sector, said: 'it is certainly appropriate to evaluate the potential environmental risks posed by medicinal products prior to their authorisation' and to monitor their effect 'when there is evidence that a substance may pose a risk to the environment'.

However, EFPIA warns that any proposed measures must be 'cost-effective, proportionate and appropriate'.

Chlorinated cocktails

Turning to the upcoming reform of the Common Agriculture Policy (CAP), Barth underlined that farm subsidies need to be linked to minimum standards of good water management.

'It is clear that at the moment water is not sufficiently addressed in the CAP,' he said, adding, however, that sustainable water management in agriculture is not only about better irrigation techniques to manage quantity.

'It is also about water quality and about how farmers use, for example, pesticides,' he said.

'While the pesticide as such could be fine, it goes through the soil, it gets degraded into other substances, ends into ground-water and finally into drinking water. Chlorinating water during the production process of drinking

I remember when you had to try hard to catch a fish. Now they seem to be pleased to get out of the water!

water could then result in hazardous substances,' he explained.

Indeed, chlorinating water may result in chemical reactions between the micro-pollutants in water, as chlorine itself is a chemical compound.

'Here, we really need to look at product stewardship – that not only the application of a product on the field is improved but also the pesticide as such. Water issues need to be looked at when developing pesticides,' he said.

The European Water Partnership has recently developed a standard for sustainable water management for farmers and is starting to test it with concrete farming communities.

'This can then be a tool to be applied in the CAP reform,' Barth suggested.

Updated 16 November 2010

⇨ The above information is reprinted with kind permission from EurActiv.com. Visit www.euractiv.com for more information.

© EurActiv.com PLC

Aid policy: ten facts and figures from the 2011 Millennium Development Goals Report

The 2011 Millennium Development Goals Report was released on 7 July with a generally upbeat assessment accompanied by some caveats. Here are some statistics.

⇨ The poverty reduction goal can be met by 2015, with the number of people in developing countries living on less than US$1.25 a day expected to fall below 900 million (from 1.8 billion in 1990).

⇨ Sub-Saharan Africa has made the greatest strides in primary school enrolment, from 58 per cent in 1999 to 76 per cent in 2009; however, 32 million children are still out of school in the region, almost half the global total of 67 million.

⇨ The number of women in parliament is at a record high – 19.3 per cent from 11.6 per cent in 1995; Rwanda, Sweden, South Africa and Cuba topped the list. Belize, the Federated States of Micronesia, Nauru, Oman, Palau, Qatar, Saudi Arabia, Solomon Islands and Tuvalu have no female parliamentarians at all.

⇨ In all regions, a mother's education is key to determining whether her children will turn five, with a child's chances of survival rising markedly with a mother's secondary or higher education.

⇨ While the demand for family planning will likely increase, in line with rising numbers of women and men of reproductive age, funding for such programmes has actually declined over the past decade, to 2.6 per cent of total aid for health in 2009.

⇨ The use of insecticide-treated mosquito nets has surged, particularly in Africa: between 2008 and 2010, 290 million nets were distributed in Sub-Saharan Africa, covering 76 per cent of the 765 million people at risk.

⇨ Water resources are no longer sustainable in Western Asia and Northern Africa, which have exceeded the 75 per cent limit on sustainable use. Southern Asia and the Caucasus and Central Asia are at rates of 58 and 56 per cent, respectively, compared with three per cent in Sub-Saharan Africa.

⇨ Latin America and the Caribbean, Eastern and South-Eastern Asia have met the target of halving the proportion of the population without sustainable access to potable water. Coverage in Sub-Saharan Africa rose from 49 per cent in 1990 to 60 per cent in 2008.

⇨ By the end of 2010, global mobile phone coverage was 76 per cent, with mobile penetration at about 68 per cent in developing countries. However, Internet penetration was as low as three per cent in the least developed countries, compared with 21 per cent in developing countries and 72 per cent in developed regions.

⇨ Donor aid is likely to increase, but at a much slower pace – two per cent between 2011 and 2013, compared with an average eight per cent per year over the past three years. Aid to Africa is expected to rise by just one per cent in real terms, against an average of 13 per cent over the past three years.

7 July 2011

⇨ The above information is reprinted with kind permission from IRIN. Visit www.irinnews.org for more information.

© IRIN 2011

EURACTIV.COM / IRIN

⇨ The environment is the complex set of physical, geographic, biological, social, cultural and political conditions that surround an individual or organism and that ultimately determine its form and the nature of its survival. (page 1)

⇨ Many organisations are searching for ways to use natural resources so they last our lifetimes and remain available for generations to come. (page 2)

⇨ Living sustainably means balancing our consumption, our technology choices and our population numbers in order to live within the resources of the planet. (page 5)

⇨ UK climate projections predict increasing summer temperatures and higher incidences of extreme weather such as heatwaves. (page 6)

⇨ Nature provides humans with all the resources necessary for life, including: energy for heat, electricity and mobility; metals for high-tech equipment; wood for furniture and paper products; construction materials for our roads and houses, and food and water for a healthy diet. (page 7)

⇨ An ESRC survey has shown that women are more likely than men to adopt pro-environmental behaviours: for example, they are four per cent more likely, on average, to be willing to pay more for environmentally-friendly products. (page 9)

⇨ Reserves of fossil fuels are being exhausted and global warming, caused by carbon dioxide emissions, is beginning to impact on our everyday lives. (page 10)

⇨ Around 40% of waste from households is currently recycled, as of 2011, compared to 11% in 2000/01. (page 12)

⇨ The Earth's population is using the equivalent of 1.5 planets' worth of natural resources, but the long-term decline of animal life appears to have been halted, a WWF report shows. (page 13)

⇨ Europe's biodiversity is heavily influenced by human activities including agriculture, forestry and fisheries, as well as urbanisation. Roughly half of Europe's land area is farmed, most forests are exploited, and natural areas are increasingly fragmented by urban areas and infrastructural development. (page 18)

⇨ In 2007, the IPCC announced that the planet has warmed about 0.75 degrees Celsius since the beginning of the 20th century. It said there is a greater than 90 per cent chance that global warming over the last 50 years is due to human activity. (page 19)

⇨ Seas and oceans absorb 25% of global carbon emissions from human activity and UK seas contain rich and varied wildlife with over 8,000 species represented. (page 22)

⇨ While the rate of population growth has slowed in most parts of the world, overall growth continues. We increase by nearly 80 million people every year. (page 26)

⇨ Current trends suggest we can expect a growing population in the UK – fuelled by increasing life expectancy and net inward migration – and an increasing number of households, more of them occupied by only one person. (page 28)

⇨ The achievement of providing 1.8 billion people with access to safe drinking water since 1990 is diminished by the absence of matching investment in sanitation. The lack of hygienic facilities experienced by 2.6 billion people is a fundamental cause of disease which leads to 1.4 million child deaths each year. (page 31)

⇨ Under pressure from rising populations, more extravagant lifestyles, intensive agriculture and industrialisation, water has become a scarce resource. (page 33)

⇨ The UK has less available water per person than most other European countries. London is drier than Istanbul, and the south-east of England has less water available per person than the Sudan and Syria. (page 34)

⇨ 884 million people in the world do not have access to safe water. This is roughly one in eight of the world's population. (page 36)

⇨ The poverty reduction goal can be met by 2015, with the number of people in developing countries living on less than US$1.25 a day expected to fall below 900 million (from 1.8 billion in 1990). (page 39)

⇨ The number of people in developing countries living on less than US$1.25 a day expected to fall below 900 million by 2015. (page 39)

Biodiversity

The number and variety of organisms found in a specific area. A balanced, healthy ecosystem will support a large number of species, making it rich in biodiversity. Human impact on the environment (for example pollution or deforestation) can reduce biodiversity, causing negative effects on the ecosystem.

Climate change

Climate change describes a global change in the balance of energy absorbed and emitted into the atmosphere. This imbalance can be triggered by natural or human processes. It can cause either regional or global variations in weather averages and frequency of severe climatic events.

Ecosystem

An ecological community comprising a complex set of relationships between all resident organisms and their habitat.

Environment

The complex set of physical, geographic, biological, social, cultural and political conditions that surround an individual or organism and that ultimately determine its form and the nature of its survival.

E-waste

Electronic waste; discarded electrical items such as mobile phones and computers. There are strict EU regulations in place to ensure that e-waste is safely recycled or disposed of: however, the shipping of e-waste to developing countries is becoming an increasingly common problem.

Global warming

This refers to a rise in global average temperatures, caused by higher levels of greenhouse gases entering the atmosphere. Global warming is affecting the Earth in a number of ways, including melting the polar ice caps, which in turn is leading to rising sea levels.

Infrastructure

The basic, interrelated systems and services needed to underpin a community or society, such as transport and the provision of power and communication systems, as well as public institutions such as schools.

Landfill

A type of waste disposal in which solid waste is buried underground, between layers of dirt. Biodegradable products will eventually break down and be absorbed into the soil: however, non-biodegradable products such as plastic carrier bags will not break down (or will do so very, very slowly).

Pollution

Toxic substances which are released into the environment: for example, harmful gases or chemicals deposited into the atmosphere or oceans. They can have a severe negative impact on the local environment, and in large quantities, on a global scale.

Recycling

The conversion of waste into new products and materials: this reduces the use of raw materials. For example, waste office paper can be recycled by pulping and processing it to make new office paper, thereby avoiding the need to obtain fresh raw materials.

Resource consumption

The use of the Earth's natural supplies, including fossil fuels, water, wood, metals, minerals and many others. Growing populations and increased standards of living have resulted in increased consumption of natural resources, which is having a negative effect on the environment.

Sanitation

Sanitation is the disposal of human sewage. Inadequate sanitation within a community can lead to disease and polluted drinking water.

Sustainability

Sustainability means living within the limits of the planet's resources to meet humanity's present-day needs without compromising those of future generations. Sustainable living should maintain a balanced and healthy environment.

Water scarcity

A lack of access to fresh drinking water. This is often a major problem for communities in regions with very arid climates, such as Sub-Saharan Africa.

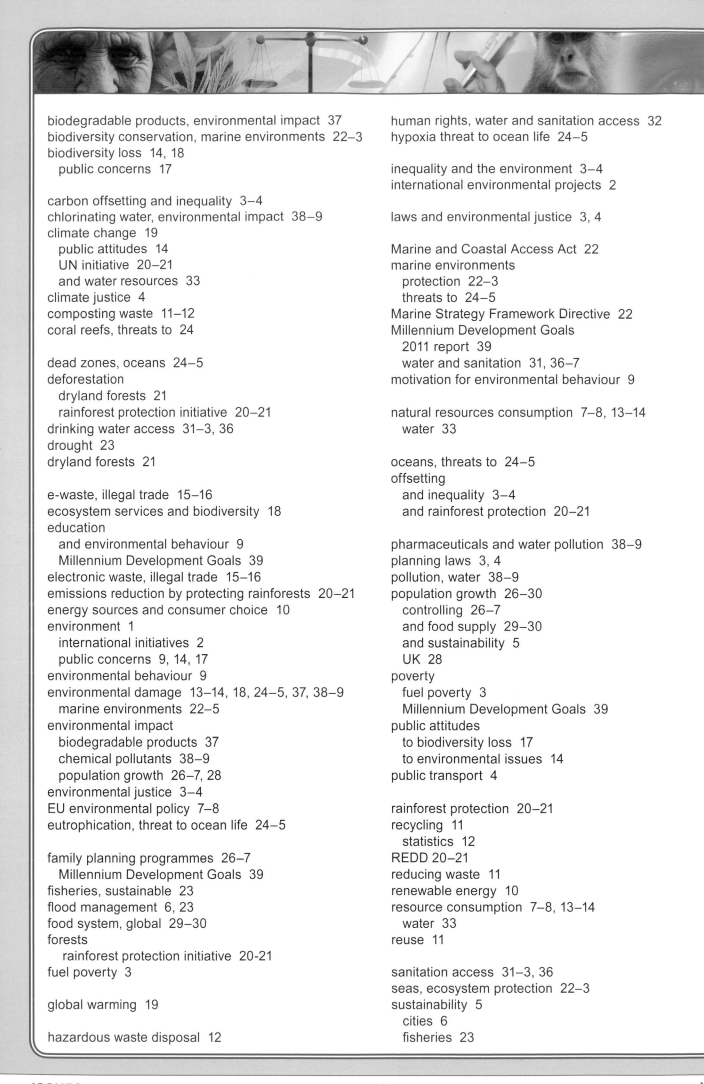

ACKNOWLEDGEMENTS

The publisher is grateful for permission to reproduce the following material.

While every care has been taken to trace and acknowledge copyright, the publisher tenders its apology for any accidental infringement or where copyright has proved untraceable. The publisher would be pleased to come to a suitable arrangement in any such case with the rightful owner.

Chapter One: Sustainable Resources

The environment, © The World Bank, *Environmental justice*, © Friends of the Earth, *Sustainability*, © Population Matters, *Sustainability and the city*, © Scottish Environment Protection Agency, *Resources and consumption*, © Friends of the Earth Europe, *When it comes to the environment, education affects our actions*, © Economic and Social Research Council, *Environmentalism, energy and consumer choice*, © The Science Museum, *Waste and recycling: a quick guide*, © Crown copyright is reproduced with the permission of Her Majesty's Stationery Office, *Waste and recycling*, © Crown copyright is reproduced with the permission of Her Majesty's Stationery Office, *Western lifestyles plundering tropics at record rate, WWF report shows*, © Guardian News and Media Limited, *Energy security is a top concern for Brits*, © Ipsos MORI, *Scandal of UK's illegal e-waste trade exposed*, © Environmental Investigation Agency.

Chapter Two: Safeguarding the Natural World

Attitudes of Europeans towards the issue of biodiversity, © European Union, *Biodiversity loss degrades natural capital and ecosystem services*, © European Environment Agency, *A history of climate change*, © Crown copyright is reproduced with the permission of Her Majesty's Stationery Office, *REDD herring*, © Ethical Consumer, *Forgotten forests have vital role in keeping deserts at bay*, © CIWEM, *The marine environment*, © Crown copyright is reproduced with the permission of Her Majesty's Stationery Office, *Floods and droughts*, © Global Water Partnership, *'Shocking' new report confirms threats to world's oceans and reefs*, © World Resources Institute.

Chapter Three: People and the Environment

Population and the environment: where we're headed and what we can do, © Population Action International, *Demographic change and the environment*, © Crown copyright is reproduced with the permission of Her Majesty's Stationery Office, *Urgent action needed to redesign the food system due to the world's growing population*, © Crown copyright is reproduced with the permission of Her Majesty's Stationery Office, *Water and sanitation*, © OneWorld UK, *Reducing water wastage in the UK*, © Waterwise, *Water statistics*, © Water Aid, *Biodegradable products may be bad for the environment*, © North Carolina State University, *Rising tide of drugs and medicines polluting EU waters*, © EurActiv.com PLC, *Aid policy: ten facts and figures from the 2011 Millennium Development Goals Report*, © IRIN.

Illustrations

Pages 1, 5, 22 and 30: Angelo Madrid; pages 2, 8, 29 and 38: Don Hatcher; pages 4, 15, 25 and 34: Simon Kneebone; pages 3 and 10: Bev Aisbett.

Cover photography

Left: © Alex Drahon. Centre: © Leonardini. Right: © Fülöp Lóránt.

Additional acknowledgements

Editorial by Carolyn Kirby on behalf of Independence.

With thanks to the Independence team: Mary Chapman, Sandra Dennis and Jan Sunderland.

Lisa Firth
Cambridge
January, 2012

ASSIGNMENTS

The following tasks aim to help you think through the debate surrounding sustainability and the environment and provide a better understanding of the topic.

1 Friends of the Earth is a charity which promotes environmental sustainability. Visit their website at www.foe.org. What sort of work do they do? List some of their campaigns and achievements.

2 Write a list of all the resources you would use during a typical school day. Try to record every material you would use, including electricity, water, food, metals, wood and anything else which occurs to you. For example, you might start with the products you use to wash with in the morning: water and electricity from the shower, the material from which your towel is made, etc. Are you surprised by just how many resources you use throughout a normal day?

3 Give a ten-minute presentation to your class on a specific energy source which is an alternative to fossil fuels. You should explain how the energy is produced and its advantages and disadvantages. Include an assessment of how economically viable the source is, how efficient it is and whether it has any negative effects on the local environment.

4 Biodiversity loss is a major concern for many individuals and organisations. But why does the loss of species matter? What effect does it have on the environment? Write an article explaining the impact of biodiversity loss and why it is significant.

5 Design an A3 wall poster entitled *What is global climate change?*. You will need to include the causes and effects of global climate change: for example, migration.

6 Beach tourism has many detrimental effects on the natural coastal environment. Imagine you are a fisherman in a developing country. You are able to make far more money transporting tourists out to coral reefs for snorkelling trips than you would ever make from fishing. What would you decide to do? Can you see the link between environmental issues and social/economic problems?

7 Read *Water statistics* on page 36. Design a promotional leaflet for the organisation which publicises the work they do and raises awareness of the ongoing water and sanitation crisis in the developing world. Pick out several key facts and statistics from the article which you think would have an impact on your readers and use them to highlight the extent of the crisis. Your leaflet should be suitable for distribution in educational institutions such as schools and libraries.

8 Is our rapidly-growing population the main cause of global environmental problems? Or is it our resource consumption and lifestyles? If population growth continued at the same rate, but global resource consumption was drastically reduced, would we still have a problem? What do you think should be done to salvage the world's rapidly diminishing resources? Discuss these issues in small groups.

9 Watch the 2004 film 'The Day After Tomorrow', starring Dennis Quaid. How does the film explore the issue of climate change? Do you think sensationalised 'blockbuster' films such as this are a good way of appealing to the public imagination and raising awareness of the problem of global warming?

10 Many people in developing countries have to walk long distances to fetch and carry water. Design a water-transportation device which would be easy to carry, lightweight and have a large storage capacity. What materials would you use? It will, of course, need to be waterproof, and resilient enough to bear a heavy load. Compare your design ideas with other students in your class.

11 Create a factsheet about the local environment surrounding your home. Include both natural and man-made elements, such as forests, rivers, power stations or industrial areas. Do you think there is much pollution in the area? Is it biodiverse? Write an article summarising your discoveries (you may also include photographs with your article if you wish).

12 Read and review 'Stark' by Ben Elton. To what extent do you think industry can be blamed for environmental problems?